W9-ATP-427

MODERN NOVELISTS

General Editor: Norman Page

MODERN NOVELISTS

Published titles

ALBERT CAMUS Philip Thody
FYODOR DOSTOEVSKY Peter Conradi
WILLIAM FAULKNER David Dowling
GUSTAVE FLAUBERT David Roe
E. M. FORSTER Norman Page
WILLIAM GOLDING James Gindin
GRAHAM GREENE Neil McEwan
HENRY JAMES Alan Bellringer
DORIS LESSING Ruth Whittaker
MALCOLM LOWRY Tony Bareham
MARCEL PROUST Philip Thody
BARBARA PYM Michael Cotsell
SIX WOMEN NOVELISTS Merryn Williams
JOHN UPDIKE Judie Newman
EVELYN WAUGH Jacqueline McDonnell
H. G. WELLS Michael Draper

Forthcoming titles

JOSEPH CONRAD Owen Knowles
F. SCOTT FITZGERALD John S. Whitley
JAMES JOYCE Richard Brown
D. H. LAWRENCE G. M. Hyde
GEORGE ORWELL Valerie Meyers
PAUL SCOTT G. K. Das
MURIEL SPARK Norman Page
GERTRUDE STEIN Shirley Neuman
VIRGINIA WOOLF Edward Bishop

MODERN NOVELISTS

GUSTAVE FLAUBERT

David Roe

St. Martin's Press   New York

All rights reserved. For information, write:
Scholarly and Reference Division,
St. Martin's Press, Inc., 175 Fifth Avenue, New York, NY 10010

First published in the United States of America in 1989

Printed in Hong Kong

Library of Congress Cataloging-in-Publication Data
Roe, David, 1943–
Gustave Flaubert / David Roe.
p. cm. – (Modern novelists)
Bibliography: p.
1. Flaubert, Gustave, 1821–1880–
Criticism and interpretation. I. Title. II. Series.
PQ2249.R63 1989   843'.8–dc19   88–24029
ISBN 0–312–02446–0: $35.00 (est.)

Contents

Note on References

In accordance with the general policy of the series, references to Flaubert's works are limited to Chapter (e.g. VIII) or Part and Chapter (e.g. I, iii) numbers. Many references are also made to Flaubert's published *Correspondance* which has had several editions. Wherever possible references are given (as, e.g. II, 123, or Sup. I, 123) to volume and page in the Conard edition (9 volumes and 4 Supplements, 1926-54). A few (as, e.g. Plé. I, 123) are taken from the newest edition, published by la Pléiade, which has only reached 1858. All translations are my own.

Acknowledgments

I am grateful to Professor Norman Page for his helpful criticism of my text and his constructive suggestions for improving it; and to my wife for making the manuscript both legible and readable.

General Editor's Preface

The death of the novel has often been announced, and part of the secret of its obstinate vitality must be its capacity for growth, adaptation, self-renewal and even self-transformation: like some vigorous organism in a speeded-up Darwinian ecosystem, it adapts itself quickly to a changing world. War and revolution, economic crisis and social change, radically new ideologies such as Marxism and Freudianism, have made this century unprecedented in human history in the speed and extent of change, but the novel has shown an extraordinary capacity to find new forms and techniques and to accommodate new ideas and conceptions of human nature and human experience, and even to take up new positions on the nature of fiction itself.

In the generations immediately preceding and following 1914, the novel underwent a radical redefinition of its nature and possibilities. The present series of monographs is devoted to the novelists who created the modern novel and to those who, in their turn, either continued and extended, or reacted against and rejected, the traditions established during that period of intense exploration and experiment. It includes a number of those who lived and wrote in the nineteenth century but whose innovative contribution to the art of fiction makes it impossible to ignore them in any account of the origins of the modern novel; it also includes the so-called 'modernists' and those who in the mid- and late twentieth century have emerged as outstanding practitioners of this genre. The scope is, inevitably, international; not only, in the migratory and exile-haunted world of our century, do writers refuse to heed national frontiers – 'English' literature lays claim to Conrad the Pole, Henry James the American, and Joyce the Irishman – but geniuses such as Flaubert, Dostoevski and Kafka have had an influence on the fiction of many nations.

Each volume in the series is intended to provide an introduction to the fiction of the writer concerned, both for those approaching him or her for the first time and for those who are already familiar with some parts of the achievement in question and now wish to place it in the context of the total *oeuvre*. Although essential information relating to the writer's life and times is given, usually in an opening chapter, the approach is primarily critical and the emphasis is not upon 'background' or generalisations but upon close examination of important texts. Where an author is notably prolific, major texts have been selected for detailed attention but an attempt has also been made to convey, more summarily, a sense of the nature and quality of the author's work as a whole. Those who want to read further will find suggestions in the select bibliography included in each volume. Many novelists are, of course, not only novelists but also poets, essayists, biographers, dramatists, travel writers and so forth; many have practised shorter forms of fiction; and many have written letters or kept diaries that constitute a significant part of their literary output. A brief study cannot hope to deal with all these in detail, but where the shorter fiction and the non-fictional writings, public and private, have an important relationship to the novels, some space has been devoted to them.

NORMAN PAGE

1
Life

Gustave Flaubert was born on December 12, 1821, in Rouen, already one of France's largest and liveliest cities; a major port and a rising industrial centre with a considerable cultural life. He grew up in a house attached to the Hôtel Dieu, or central hospital, of which his father was surgeon-in-chief. His elder brother Achille, born in 1813, became a doctor and succeeded their father in the post.

The family was rich and well-respected in the city, and Gustave had a happy and comfortable childhood, enjoying a close and protective relationship with his younger sister Caroline. However, suffering, disease and death were never far away. Not only could he watch operations and autopsies from his home, but the family was badly scarred by the early deaths of three other children, and the delicate health of both Gustave and Caroline was at first a cause of concern.

Gustave soon grew stronger, and began to show a precocious interest in literature. At the age of ten he was compiling little plays for the family's makeshift theatre, in collaboration with Ernest Chevalier. This was the first of a series of intimate male friendships, rooted in literature, which were to be a major feature of his life. At eleven he entered the Collège Royal (grammar school). He was a voracious reader and his studies, especially of history, progressed steadily, while teachers encouraged his writing.

Influenced by the new historical drama of the French Romantics, by Shakespeare and Walter Scott, he wrote more elaborate plays. But he also turned to fiction, with cynical or satanic tales, stories of the fantastic (one was published locally in 1837) and occasional stories of modern life, including the first of many satirical portraits ('The Office Clerk', also published) and his first account of a provincial adultery, based on a case read in a newspaper.

Dr Flaubert was a pioneer exponent of the tonic qualities of the

1

seaside, and the family spent summer holidays at Trouville, then a tiny fishing village. In 1836 Gustave met there Elisa Foucault, the twenty-six year old mistress of a Paris music publisher, Maurice Schlesinger. A long tradition has held that he immediately conceived a deep but hopeless Romantic passion for her which was to cast its shadow over the whole of his adult life and haunt his fiction. The lack of any direct evidence of Flaubert's feelings in 1836–7 has made recent scholars more circumspect. He may have been more affected by an English girl, Caroline Herland, whom he met in 1837. However, she married in January 1838, and when later that year he evoked both women in his autobiographical story *Mémoires d'un Fou* (Memoirs of a Madman), the Elisa-inspired character, called Maria, was given the major role, though the narrator insisted that his love for her was retrospective, born during a later visit to the same resort in her absence.

Neither relationship was portrayed as progressing very far, and personal reminiscences blended into Gustave's new conventional stance of gloomy pessimism. He had come under the influence of an older friend, the Byronic poet Alfred Le Poittevin, who was obsessed by metaphysical questions, such as the problem of evil, to which, like so many of his generation, he could not accept religious answers. Death, the devil, the nothingness of disappointed existences, became the centre of Gustave's literary preoccupations, and his philosophical ambitions are reflected in *Smarh*, the first of a series of long and lavish treatments of the theme of philosophical and metaphysical temptation. While Satan reveals all to a sincere hermit, his follower Yuk incarnates Gustave's view that cynical laughter is man's only weapon in the face of an absurd universe. Though derivative, *Smarh* was a sincere statement of Gustave's position, and on completing it in April 1839, he even felt discouraged from continuing to write. He freely acknowledged that the comforts of his material life were at odds with his inner unhappiness and spiritual void (I,46). Having decided that 'Vanity is the basis of everything' (I,39), that he would complete his studies but not take up a career, he saw his future role as 'thinker and demoraliser': 'I will do no more than tell the truth, but it will be horrible, cruel and naked.' (I,41).

In December 1839 he was expelled from school for leading a rebellion against what he saw as administrative malpractice: an early example of his fierce independence of spirit and contempt for authority. Studying privately, he passed the *baccalauréat* in August 1840, thus qualifying for university education. His father sent him on a tour of southern France and Corsica for two months with Dr Cloquet, one of his pupils. His interest in Classical history was intensified by such impressive Roman remains as the arena at Nimes, where he could almost hear the shouts of the crowds. He was fascinated too by the savagery and the strange code of honour of Corsica. His first sight of the Mediterranean awakened a desire to cross it to visit North Africa or the Middle East.

Passing through Marseilles on his return, he had a brief but intense physical relationship with the thirty-five year old Eulalie Foucaud de Langlade, a friend of his companion. The theme of the discovery of sensual love was to recur frequently in his fiction, though he usually attributed it to women characters. Eulalie herself wrote him passionate letters, but they never met again. He made several pilgrimages to her former house (she had moved to America) and remembered her with some warmth, but she seems not to have had the lasting effect on his emotions and imagination which his correspondence, and the conception of his third mature novel, *L'Education Sentimentale*, attribute to Elisa.

Little is known of Gustave's occupations in 1841. His parents were anxious for him to continue his studies and enter a profession, while he apparently remained interested only in art and self-analysis, with little faith that he would progress in either. He finally registered at the Paris Law Faculty in November, and made occasional visits to the capital: an attitude to study by no means unusual at the time. He wrote to a former teacher that he had ideas for three totally different novels, each requiring its own style (I,95); and he made it clear to friends that he had no intention of practising law, though he possessed one major courtroom asset, a strong and sonorous voice, which he was to use subsequently to good literary effect in reading out his works as he composed them.

He spent the early summer of 1842 cramming for his exams, but seems to have been barred from taking them by a professor exasperated at student absenteeism. After a holiday in Trouville he returned to Paris for the new academic year, attended lectures and passed a first exam in December. He also led an active social life, visiting Schlesinger, now married to Elisa, and the Colliers, an English family he had met at Trouville. He probably flirted with Gertrude (twenty-three) and Henrietta (eighteen), and some suspect that he may have gone further with Elisa Schlesinger; for he was at this time athletically handsome as well as cultivated and witty.

He also struck up a close friendship with an ambitious young writer, Maxime du Camp. He found Law hard and unrewarding, could not take the concept of Justice seriously, and, more interested in the composition of a long psychological novel, duly failed his next exam in August 1843. The novel is built round the opposition between two friends, the thrusting and ambitious Henry and the introspective budding writer Jules. Both will be disappointed in love, but while Henry finally succeeds in business, Jules achieves a greater breakthrough, in Gustave's eyes, reaching a complex if ill-defined vision of the writer's role and function, rooted in a distanced contemplation of the world.

The composition of this novel, completed early in 1845, bridges a key experience in Gustave's life, which probably affected the lessons its later pages drew. In early January 1844, while travelling from Pont l'Evéque to Honfleur with his brother, he was struck down by a mysterious seizure, probably epileptic and perhaps brought on by his reluctance to continue his studies. He recovered sufficiently to return to Paris in the middle of the month, but a second attack came in Rouen a week or so later. This time Dr Flaubert imposed a strict diet and a prolonged convalescence. He purchased a house on the river to the west of Rouen, at Croisset: it was to be Gustave's home and retreat for the rest of his life. Further attacks followed, and the family accepted that he would not be able to resume his studies or consider a professional career. There was substantial investment income, so Gustave would not need to work: a fact which was to prove as crucial as the illness itself, for barring accidents, and unlike most major authors of the century, he would never have to write for money. Gustave saw the change in his prospects in extreme terms. He wrote that the illness had ended his exterior life and begun an exclusively inner life of thinking, observing and creating (I, 277-8). With all pressure to conform removed, he was quite happy to remain in Normandy, writing when his attacks allowed. He had come back under the influence of Le Poittevin, whose pessimism the more robust du Camp struggled unsuccessfully to counter, for the events of the next two years seemed to reinforce the poet's gloomy message.

In March 1845, his sister Caroline married Emile Hamard, and the whole family joined the honeymoon trip to Italy, a journey over-shadowed by her deteriorating health. There were some pleasures for Gustave: contemplation of the sea or lakes, study of the great painters. Above all there was the crucial illumination before Breughel's picture of *The Temptation of Saint Antony*: the theme was to haunt him for thirty years as he struggled to retell the story in words. In the autumn, as Caroline was nursed through a precarious pregnancy, Dr Flaubert himself fell ill.

He died on January 15, 1846, six days before the birth of his grand-daughter Caroline, and ten weeks before the death of his daughter. Gustave's oldest friend, Chevalier, was no longer at hand to support him, having moved to Corsica, while in July Le Poittevin married a Mademoiselle de Maupassant and left Rouen. It was thus almost on a rebound and out of a need to forget his griefs, that on one of his regular trips to Paris he flung himself into an affair with Louise Colet, a married thirty-six year old beauty, poetess and mistress of the philosopher Victor Cousin. He assured her that she was the first woman he had both loved and physically possessed (Plé. I, 279). But the relationship between two strong-willed individuals of otherwise opposed temperaments and literary ideals could only be stormy. Rows and reconciliations alternated until March 1848, generating a significant correspondence. When Louise announced she was expecting a child by her husband, Gustave seized the opportunity to escape.

Louise had not occupied the whole of his existence. He had formed a close friendship with another Rouennais writer, his former schoolfellow Louis Bouilhet, who was earning his living by giving classes. He had a high regard for Bouilhet's poetry and plays and his literary judgement, submitting his own writings to the poet for detailed comment. Though his illness was not yet overcome, he made a long tour of the Loire Valley and Brittany with du Camp between May and August, 1847, covering many of the miles on foot. A long travel book, written jointly, remained in manuscript. As the year drew to a close unrest and political instability grew. Flaubert had shown little interest in politics and he watched with ironic curiosity the February Revolution bring down the 'bourgeois' monarchy of Louis-Philippe. Though glad to see it go, he had a congenital aversion to the common people which made Republican democracy no more attractive. He was more disturbed by the death, a few weeks later, of Le Poittevin.

Under the influence of younger literary friends he had been ready to move away from the poet's Romantic manner if not, fundamentally, from his nihilistic pessimism, but in his grief he lurched back. He had for some time been gathering material for his St Antony project, and now began work on the text. He wrote intensively for eighteen months, adopting the once-popular form of the unstageable philosophical ddrama. But Le Poittevin's brand of 'disenchanted' and satanic writing was now out of fashion. Poetry had moved on to more controlled forms, stressing plastic values, while prose was dominated by the realistic novel of modern life, exemplified by the works of Balzac (who died in 1850). When he read his immense manuscript to Bouilhet and du Camp – it took four days! – they were most discouraging. Though profoundly disappointed, he bore them no ill-will and was soon off with du Camp to realise his dream of seeing the Middle East. During his eighteen-month tour he discovered the reality behind the poetic images: life there, too, could be coarse, dirty, brutal and uncivilised. He spent time in Cairo, sailed up the Nile to see the great temples, crossed the desert by camel, visited the Holy Land, Beirut, Rhodes and Constantinople, and paused briefly in Greece and Naples on the journey home. Although proud of the way he had risen to the physical challlenges, he returned to France in June 1851 prematurely aged. He was balding, fat and nursing the after-effects of syphilis.

While travelling, he had intermittently wondered what to write next. Projects ranged from the satirical to the Romantic and potentially self-indulgent, from a collection of clichés to be called 'Dictionary of Received Ideas' to a novel on the theme of unsatisfiable desire, perhaps with Don Juan as hero. On his return to Rouen he took up instead the story of a former pupil of his father's, Delamare, his two wives and early death, and wove around it an elaborate network of more down-to-earth themes. He had spent much time on his travels observing people, places and things, and seeking to describe them with precision in his letters and journals. His new work would exploit this skill. Although he began writing on his name day, the 16th September, he had no intention of locking himself away in Croisset permanently. He visited the Great Exhibition in London that autumn, and was in Paris when Louis-Napoleon seized power in December. He witnessed some of the street violence which ushered in the Second Empire, a period of stifling conformity and bad taste that was to bring him many aesthetic and intellectual frustrations and irritations. His personal affairs also promised little serenity. Louise Colet, far from forgetting him, had come to see him as the most important of all her lovers and, flattered by her renewed attentions but failing to grasp the intensity of feelings they betokened, he allowed the affair to restart. He was generally more successful this time at controlling the relationship, keeping her a comfortable train-journey from Croisset, where he spent weekdays painstakingly writing *Madame Bovary* and weekends discussing with Bouilhet the few pages he had just written.

Writing is a difficult and demanding art, he repeatedly told Louise, whose spontaneous sentimental and confessional approach made her a curiously unsuitable audience for his endless explorations of a new aesthetic of prose and a new concept of the novel. Nor did she appreciate the hours of patiently constructive criticism he lavished on her own works, driving home his messages of emotional detachment and careful composition; especially as he was far more reluctant to lavish time and attention on her person. Nevertheless, now widowed and hoping he would finally marry her, Louise clung on until 1854. Even after a brief affair with the poet Vigny, she made a further effort early in 1855; a curt note dismissed her for ever. She took her revenge by portraying him in her novels and poems as a cruel and unfeeling lover. Although the affair with Louise seems to indicate that he had broken the spell cast over his emotional life since the later 1830s by Elisa Schlesinger, it also shows the limits of his capacity for commitment to love, limits he had never ceased to spell out to Louise during their relationship. After it, there would be no more such passions, though during the 1850s he flirted – and perhaps more – with his niece's English governesses, which did not prevent him from taking a serious active interest in Caroline's education.

Later he may have had short affairs with actresses and literary women in Paris. But he also managed to find other women willing to stop short at the intellectual friendship he offered, and to listen to, or read, the outpouring of his ideas. For from 1850 he developed two totally opposed ways of writing and thinking; the meticulous, for his literary works, and the spontaneous, for his correspondence. A week at Croisset might produce a page of fiction but dozens of pages of letters. The sense of release as he changed modes spilled over into vigorous and at times unbridled vocabulary and imagery, or the quickfire sequence of maxims and generalisations which his new principle of authorial silence, so different from the opinionated garrulity of earlier novelists, had banished from his fiction.

Madame Bovary was completed to his satisfaction in April 1856 and published serially in du Camp's periodical *La Revue de Paris* between October and December. The Empire had developed decidedly Victorian views on artistic taste and licence, especially where it suspected the coexistence of moral and political liberalism. Du Camp and his collaborators, already politically suspect, proceeded cautiously with Flaubert's novel of provincial adultery, asking for cuts, then infuriating him by making fresh ones without warning. He finally insisted that the Review publish a note in which he disclaimed any responsibility for the incomplete state of the serial text. Despite the editor's efforts, they and the author were prosecuted for outrage to morals and religion. Flaubert, who was not quite so unworldly as he liked to appear, mobilised a considerable lobby, but failed to prevent the case coming to trial. The prosecution was inept, while the defence, well-primed by the author, missed no opportunity to stress the novel's serious purpose and its scrupulous respect for truth, as when contested passages on religion were shown to be based on texts approved by the Church. Though the charges were not upheld, the judge permitted himself a weighty criticism of the 'misuse' of Art. When the text appeared in volume form, in April 1857, a *succès de scandale* was assured, and Flaubert regretted having sold the rights for a few hundred francs. Critical praise, however, was generally ill-directed, only the poet Baudelaire grasping that the main thrust of the work was to be sought in the rôle of the heroine rather than the subtitle theme 'Provincial Manners' which more conveniently fitted into current trends in the novel and hence in critical pigeonholing.

Flaubert had not been idle since the spring of 1856. He had reworked *La Tentation de Saint Antoine*, reduced it to less than half its original length, and published extracts. But the prosecution of *Madame Bovary* discouraged him from risking the full publication of a book which offered a sceptical view of the development of world religions, and dwelt on sexual temptations. He collected material on the legend of St Julian the Hospitaller, the theme of a window in Rouen Cathedral, but abandoned the idea for a subject chosen in the more obscure pages of the history of Carthage, Ancient Rome's rival for the dominance of the Mediterranean. It offered a compromise between the realism of *Madame Bovary* (he could scrupulously document himself on the 'manners' of the time) and the imaginative and metaphysical excesses of *La Tentation*. Themes and settings allowed scope for luxuriant description, extremes of character and action, and a metaphysical dimension rooted in Mediterranean mythologies. He visited the ancient sites in Tunisia in 1858. Though Croisset remained his writing retreat, he now spent more time in Paris, supporting Bouilhet's burgeoning career in the theatre and cultivating the new circle of friends and admirers brought by his first book. His initial confidence that the second novel would be dashed off in a year or so soon evaporated, and five years once more proved necessary for the process of research, plans, more specialised documentation and composition.

Completed in the spring of 1862 and published in November, *Salammbô* enjoyed considerable success among the sophisticated reading public, although it was fiercely contested by some critics, historians and churchmen. Flaubert allowed himself to be drawn more fully into the social life of literary salons and even of the Imperial Court, where he became a favourite with the Emperor's intelligent and cultivated cousin Mathilde. His circle of literary friends widened, both among contemporaries like George Sand, the Goncourt brothers and the Russian novelist Turgenev, who had settled in France, and among younger writers such as Zola and Daudet.

After some hesitation he had chosen as the subject of his next novel the young men of his generation and the Paris of the 1840s. The central plot was inspired, as his earliest sketches indicate, by aspects of his relationship with Maurice and Elisa Schlesinger, but the strong personal element was accompanied by the customary meticulous planning and research, and five more years of his life were swallowed up, the last page being written on May 16, 1869. The final revisions had to be made this time without the valued advice of Bouilhet, gravely ill. His death in July, followed by that of the critic Sainte-Beuve in October, cast a shadow over the publication of *L'Education Sentimentale* in November. Though it sold quite well, it was widely criticised for political radicalism and structural shapelessness. Flaubert felt that his main points had been completely missed.

More cruel blows soon followed: the deaths of friends and colleagues (Jules Duplan, Jules de Goncourt), then the defeat of France and the Prussian occupation, a trauma to Flaubert as to many other intellectuals who had not hitherto considered themselves patriots. Paris withstood seige, but Normandy was overrun, and Flaubert was driven from Croisset between December 1870 and April 1871. There were family difficulties, too: his mother's age and ill-health, and financial problems brought by the incompetence of his nephew by marriage. When his mother died in April 1872, she left Croisset to Caroline, though he could continue to live there. He worked on, not only for himself, making a third, even slimmer version of *La Tentation*, but also for Bouilhet's reputation and his family. He tirelessly harassed the municipality of Rouen to have a memorial erected, and cajoled Paris theatre directors to put on Bouilhet's plays, including one, *Le Sexe Faible*, which he had himself worked up from a posthumous scenario. Encouraged by one of the directors he had approached, he even dashed off, in a few weeks, an original play, *Le Candidat*, a sarcastic comedy about an election in a small town. It was premiered on March 11, 1874, but was poorly received and supported, and he withdrew it after only four performances. A few weeks later the short version of *La Tentation* was published. Though the critics did not like it, it attracted enough attention to be translated into German the same year.

Flaubert's health began to deteriorate, and he spent part of the summer of 1874 in Switzerland convalescing. 1875 began with a further chapter of ailments, followed by a chapter of financial disasters for his nephew. To save him from disgrace, Flaubert sold a substantial property on the coast which had assured much of his income; he also moved to cheaper quarters for his stays in Paris. Croisset itself was saved, but thereafter the novelist constantly feared the loss of his precious retreat. He had begun a new novel, based on two old projects: the 'Dictionary of Received Ideas' of the early 1850s and an outline sketched in 1863 concerning two Paris copyists who devote their rural retirement to unsuccessful efforts to acquire knowledge. Losing confidence and patience, he abandoned the book in the summer of 1875, and turned to short fiction.

By February 1877 he had written *Trois Contes* (Three Tales), realising an ambition he had briefly held in 1856 to publish all at once a modern text (*Un Coeur simple* in this case), a medieval (*La Légende de St Julien l'Hospitalier*) and a classical (*Hérodias*). Wearing their erudition much more lightly than the novels, the stories delighted the critics. Unfortunately the general public did not buy, and Flaubert, whose unearned income had hitherto underpinned his supreme indifference to literature as commerce, badly needed the money. New editions of his works were brought out as he toiled away at *Bouvard et Pécuchet*, which he did not expect to finish before 1881. His creative imagination had never stood still during the sternly-disciplined periods of composition, and even now he was noting further projects: the battle of Thermopylae, or a major study of the Second Empire grouped round the story of a Parisian marriage.

In 1878 he was still making trips round Normandy with a young disciple, Guy de Maupassant, to verify facts for his present work. In 1879 came more bad health, more money worries, and he had to allow friends to petition for a sinecure post (a disguised pension) from the Third Republic, which he scorned as much as any of the other régimes under which he had lived. He worked on at his novel, reaching chapter ten by the end of 1880, with the final chapters already outlined. At Easter 1881, four of his greatest friends and admirers – Daudet, Goncourt, Maupassant and Zola – visited him at Croisset. A month later, more friends offered him a grand dinner. On May 8th he died suddenly of a cerebral haemorrhage. A provincial to the end, he is buried alongside his parents in the cemetery at Rouen.

2
The Early Works

Flaubert was one of those writers who, from his earliest years, could not bear to throw away any piece of paper on which he had written. Though he published virtually nothing before *Madame Bovary*, posthumous 'complete' editions of his works begin with numerous literary texts, journals of his travels and even some school exercises.[1] Indeed the line is hard to draw, in 1835–36, between school work and free composition, as the latter is dominated by themes from history, his favourite school subject. But soon he adopted the then popular form of the 'philosophical' tale, using elements of the fantastic, and at first a knowing irony, to express pessimism about human destiny, and illustrate in a colourful fashion the ultimate questions of life and death, especially death.

Romantic literature of the 1830s was full of disillusion and disenchantment, and at fourteen Gustave made these themes his own. Brought up outside the Church, he saw no reason to reject the religious scepticism – or worse – of the Byron-inspired generation. In drawing the moral of an early tale of premature burial, he invited his readers to reproach God with their bitter existence (*Rage et Impuissance*). The narrator of another tale declares his contempt for God, contrasting his own suffering existence with the eternal beauty of Nature: an opposition which will run throughout his fiction (*La Dernière Heure*). Satan clashes with a superior being which, devoid of soul or feelings, is condemned to live in eternal boredom (*Rêve d'Enfer*). A monster, half-ape half-man, kills the girl it loves but cannot communicate with, in a story notable for increased attention to precise detail, anchoring the fantasy in familiar settings (*Quidquid Volueris*, 1837).

Dramatisation of states of mind is replacing the mere illustration of ideas: a bride's reported thoughts prefigure the premarital hopes of Emma Bovary. But the narrator, in the manner of Balzac (then

12

reaching the peak of his power) is always at the reader's shoulder to comment. Thus in the more realistic *Passion et Vertu*, the fifteen-year-old disquisits knowingly on modern seducers, interjects sympathetic asides or corrects the fond illusions of his passionate heroine, while also describing her states of mind and occasionally recalling the more cosmic gloom of earlier philosopher-protagonists. Cosmic gloom returns in a chronicle-play, *Loys XI*, who emerges as yet another character haunted by death and fear of the unknown after it.

Death, damnation, the corruption of the body, the unlikelihood of God's existence, the vanity of life, the desire to escape, crowd the overheated pages of the poetic prose of 1838, at the expense of narrative framework or realism.

Personal, even autobiographical, elements enter *Mémoires d'un Fou*. In a preliminary note to Le Poittevin, Gustave confesses that though he had aimed to write just another sceptical fiction, 'little by little, as (he) wrote, the personal impression came through the fable, the soul shook the pen and crushed it'. Thus the narrator describes his earliest loves, borrowing from Gustave's own experiences with Elisa Schlesinger and Caroline Herland and adding the portrait of an unnamed woman who initiated him (and Gustave?) sexually. Later chapters abandon narrative to offer direct reflections on Art, infinity, the impossibility of free will, before returning to the seaside village to describe a later visit, when Maria (Elisa) was no longer there and when in her absence he began to love her.

Mostly at this time, the 'personal impression' did not 'come through the fable' quite so openly. *Smarh* is a blend of his earlier styles and themes in its dialogue account of Satan's temptation of a hermit whose resilience is fuelled by hope and aspiration, but whose thirst for knowledge is pitilessly exploited by the master of nihilistic logic. Forty years before *Bouvard et Pécuchet* Satan cheerfully announces that 'science is doubt, nothingness, lies, vanity'; and he shows up Man's weakness before the forces of Nature. He is accompanied by a less obviously derivative figure, Yuk, who incarnates the immortal awfulness of human life assumed with a cynical laugh. Laughter dominates another text of 1839, in which Dr Mathurin chooses to die happy, as he has lived. He looks forward to eternal sleep, confusing in a final lecture gastronomy and philosophy. Flaubert's cosmic pessimism is now expressed in the context of a derision which, even faced by death, refuses to take things tragically. If it is, in Bruneau's words[2] a farewell to

Flaubert's earliest period of meditation on the meaning of life, it is unexpectedly cheerful, prefiguring the strong comic element in the major novels.

In 1840 the corrosive adolescent scepticism finally seems to have dried up the stream of imitative fiction, though Gustave continued to reflect on Art, 'this strange translation of thought by form'.[3] His father had advised him to look and learn on his first voyage[4] and on his return he tried his hand at a travel book. Sketchy descriptions of buildings, streets, landscapes and people abound, though such concrete subjects are subordinated to the personality and inner experiences of the narrator. He also jotted down in a notebook a series of disenchanted maxims and self-analyses. He observed how one lies to oneself, even as one writes, and how language is unable to express exactly one's ideas:[5]

> There is a stupid axiom which says that words render thoughts
> – it would be more true to say that they distort them.

Yet he still made notes on the nature of writing: on the dangers of composing a work merely to prove a point, for example. He also observed in himself that longing to be someone else which, if it was not the initial impulse to create fictional characters, became in later life a valued side effect. Above all, he contrasted the abstract, over-systematic *pensée* (thought) with the freer, concrete *poésie* (poetry), which created a solid world of its own.[6] Though the function of all writers was to be thinkers, tackling the great human questions, he wanted to do it in a concrete way, not as a philosopher.

Between 1840 and the end of 1842 he managed only one work of fiction, the ninety-page story *Novembre*. Commentators share his own view of this as his earliest work of real value. The story of a mixed-up adolescent's awakening to love, sex and Nature, is told partly by the protagonist, with Romantic flourishes of pathetic fallacy, and partly by an intermittently ironic narrator. It includes the first person life-story of the prostitute who initiates the hero into sexual passion. More singlemindedly than him, she seeks a total love, not some disincarnated ideal but rooted in a satisfactory sexual partnership with a man who will also respond to her feelings and imagination. The hero is much vaguer about his goals. Plagued by Romantic *ennui* (boredom with life itself), he seeks escape through love, travel, Art and pantheistic communion with Nature. He drifts into law studies, though he has no social or professional ambitions. Unlike his creator, though, he has no drive, patience or determination, being too indecisive even to carry through the temptation to commit suicide. Whereas *Mémoires d'un Fou* is interesting mainly for its insights into the adolescent Flaubert, *Novembre* shows him building up independent fictional character and dramatic interest out of his experiences. He is not always convincing – the prostitute's literary language rings less true than her psychology – but he is trying hard. The double perspective on the hero is well handled, autobiographical material, such as the relationship with Nature, being explored in both the first and the third person, showing some capacity for 'distancing' it. An extraordinary number of the story's specific themes and motifs will recur in the mature works, from the hero's aimless roaming through Paris streets to that inversion of traditional polarities which makes the female strong and the male weak.

Next Flaubert wrote, between February 1843 and January 1845, his first full-length novel, *L'Education Sentimentale*, another study of the passage from adolescence to adulthood, and at first sight a confirmation of his move away from metaphysical questionings and extravagant literary forms to the psychological novel of modern life. Confessional narrowness is broadened by the presence of two contrasting protagonists, surrounded by a substantial cast of minor figures swiftly and often satirically etched in scenes of middle-class comedy. The 'education' is not merely the apprenticeship in love, nor even, as the French 'sentimental' implies, that of the affective life in general, but also the preparation of the material future, the adult social rôle and finally the whole intellectual and moral 'growing up'.

'The hero of this book', according to the first sentence, is Henry, a provincial youth come up to Paris to study law, bringing a typically Flaubertian unhappiness which the distractions of the capital fail to dispel. A secondary rôle is played by his school friend Jules, left behind to work in an office. He tells his own unpromising story in a series of letters. Henry gradually develops a relationship with his landlord's wife, while Jules, a budding writer, interests a theatrical troupe in one of his works, and the leading actress in himself. While Henry flees to America with his mistress to start a new life, Jules is betrayed, but emerges from the consequent Romantic despair with a detached appreciation of relative values which leads him to pursue truth and understanding through the study of history and the composition of poems. Henry's passion is short-lived, but he finds greater happiness at a lower level of intensity. He returns to France, gives up his mistress and matures into a self-satisfied mediocrity whose superficial culture helps him to sustain his place in society. Hardly Flaubert's 'hero', if he was ever intended to be!

Jules continues his solitary artistic development in parallel to Flaubert's, shaking off Romantic clichés like local colour or confessional fiction in favour of the study of history or modern life, undertaken with rigour, honesty and critical irony. Though poor and alone, he enjoys a rich inner life as he comprehends and reconstructs, transforming the example into the law. Flaubert's ideas here are as vague as the literary works of Jules that he mentions. The rise and rise of the artist, whether or not a response to the change in Flaubert's own life after January 1844, seems to unbalance the novel, whose long final chapters sacrifice narrative and drama to analysis and speculation. There is also some confusion, incoherent and rather unfinished, though deeply felt, passages on Jules sitting uneasily beside smug and even uninterested passages on the Balzacian dandy-figure that Henry has become.

Nonetheless the work deserves its recent publication in a popular edition. Flaubert shows himself capable of developing ideas, characters and narrative structure over a considerable span, and of entertaining the reader with scenes of comedy and sentimental drama. He portrays with skill the development of affections at various levels of intensity, tackling the falling out of, as well as into, love. He initiates a long series of comic portraits of the middle-class expert in received ideas; practises dialogue to excess in early chapters, and antithetical analysis likewise in the last three or four. He continues to experiment with third and first person narration, though the inherent difficulties of the letter-form cause him to abandon it a third of the way through. The omniscient narrator's voice is prominent, its maxims and metaphors recalling Balzac, its superiority over the characters, Stendhal. There is some concrete description, but portraits are on the whole moral and psychological. Towards the end the narrator notes that the shaping pattern of an individual existence is partly the product of its origins, partly of early experiences: a point to be exemplified in the exposition of *Madame Bovary*. The ultimate disequilibrium and confusion represent the emergence of the double literary self of

Flaubert,[7] offsetting the mediocre majority with a more positive view of the élite, represented by the artist. The almost playful conclusion, summarising the fates of all the characters, indicates the corollary; that the practical succeed in the world, the dreamers and thinkers fail, as will always be the case in the mature fiction.

*

In the works of the decade 1835–45, all written for himself or his closest friends, Flaubert's derivative, pessimistic vision has anchored itself in specific forms of disappointment, notably unhappy love and the revulsion from petty and materialistic 'bourgeois' values. It has shed much of its metaphysical content. *L'Education Sentimentale* projects Flaubert's own resolution to the problem of living: choose Art not as anaesthetic but as a means of knowing the world. Though a novel of the artist – Flaubert's last such, explicitly – it is not self reflective in the modern sense. Jules decides that it is too early to put modern life under the microscope, and instead of writing a modern novel resembling the one in which he figures, he plans vast poems and dramas.

Flaubert himself in 1845 projected either theatrical works or narratives set in the remote or imaginary past of the philosophical tale. What he actually wrote next blended ancient and modern, Art and reality. First came travel notes brought back from Italy. Many are telegraphic memory guides to people, places or works of Art, but some episodes, more fully worked out, show the pleasurable feeling roused by paintings or by Nature and the disgust aroused by human stupidity or ugliness. After the trip to Brittany he and du Camp prepared a detailed account.[8] Flaubert's chapters contain a lively mix of physical description, borrowed erudition and determined efforts at grasping atmosphere. The tone is sometimes respectful, sometimes amused, occasionally bitter, especially when recalling tasteless manifestations of modernity, from hats to artificial grottoes. Though indulging his love of history he writes extensively of the contemporary state of the provinces visited. Brittany was a poor backwater, and the travellers were as struck by the wretched conditions of rural life as by the tenacity of religious faith, greatly weakened elsewhere in France. They noted the prosperity of the towns, explored social phenomena, such as begging, and recorded many contrasts between Nature and culture.

Apart from this apprenticeship in detailed social observation, the most significant aspect of this work, in the context of Flaubert's development as a writer, lies in the proliferation of word pictures. Since 1840 he had learnt to see and hear, and now showed skill in etching lively scenes, accumulating details in rhythmic sequence and rounding them off with a telling image, whether to describe a timeless landscape, the proportions of a great monument or the banal clutter of a modern town.

Neither of these novelistic qualities was much in evidence in Flaubert's massive treatment of *La Tentation de Saint Antoine*. Although he told Le Poittevin in 1845 that he was considering an 'arrangement for the theatre' of Breughel's theme (Plé. I, 230), it was eventually written between May 1848 and September 1849: the first work for a decade to be intended for publication. It has the superficial appearance of a play, being divided into stage directions, monologue and dialogue. It even obeys the Classical unity of time, the action being completed, in a neat inversion of traditional practice, between sunset and sunrise. But like many other 'plays' of the Romantic period, including its models such as Goethe's *Faust* or the religious 'mysteries' of the 1830s in France, it is 'arranged' for no theatre that even a modern director could imagine. It features single speeches of ten pages with thinly disguised narrative or description, innumerable settings, instantaneous transformations and endless parades of figures representing Christian heresies, mythical animals and ancient divinities. Flaubert revels in the fantastic and exotic, as well as mythological and historical elements, while a pig, borrowed from mediaeval legend, articulates its animalistic appetites and its creator's taste for the grotesque. Yet this is also the first work Flaubert compiled from assiduous research among the best authorities, ancient and modern.[9] Narrative, description and ideas, however outlandish, are nowhere his own invention.

Needless to say, Flaubert's purpose is not hagiographic, though the third-century Egyptian Saint Antony was revered as an early model for a simple, ascetic Christianity and one of the founders of the monastic movement. The major attraction was the legend of his repeated temptations. Flaubert had sceptically but superficially illustrated the weak points of Christian doctrine in his teenage tales. He now offered a more comprehensive, though not always comprehensible survey. Antoine has chosen asceticism and solitude (like the secular artists Jules and Flaubert), but he is assailed by doubts and seeks divine reassurance. The temptations, though presented in a complicated and repetitive manner, broadly fall into the triple pattern found in Genesis or the Gospels. Antoine is tempted physically (mainly through his sexuality), psychologically (mainly through pride) and intellectually (through the personification of Logic, chipping away at the incoherences of Christianity like a disciple of the Enlightenment). The reality of Christ is argued away, good and evil shown to be relative concepts, the Devil, God's own creation. A dazzling array of heresies passes, often, as Antoine remarks, more outrageous than pagan beliefs, their varied interpretation of doctrine showing theology as absurd. Antoine is more frightened than attracted by them, but a persuasive prophet finds his weakness by offering knowledge. In a dramatic climax to Part I many hostile figures crowd back, hoping to win his soul from God.

His desperate prayers are answered by the three theological Virtues, which draw the Devil onto the stage, though for most of Part II he only directs the attacks of his minions. The Virtues are little use, since their theological definitions prevent them offering Antoine the solid certitudes he seeks. The stage confrontation with evil is interrupted, though, as if Flaubert is unwilling to give even symbolic victory to either side. The modern truth-seeker, Science, attracts Antoine, despite being clearly an enemy of faith, and with Logic and Pride (most powerful because most insidious of the Sins) it flatters Antoine's ego. A new series of conventional temptations follows, colourfully if unnecessarily offering wealth, power or sex yet again. Antoine resists even the allure of the Queen of Sheba. The coupling of a sphinx and a chimaera generates a host of strange creatures whose vivacity and variety awaken in him a desire to live in everything, 'to enter every atom, to circulate in matter, be matter myself so as to know what it thinks'.

Though Antoine's outburst is enigmatic, it marks a weakening of his faith, for the Devil advances to address him directly. In the opening pages of Part III he takes on the rôle of Spinoza-inspired explicator of Antoine's quasi-pantheistic urge. With the help of astronomy, atomic theory and echoes of Flaubert's own pantheistic experiences, he convinces Antoine that he is part of a single Divine Substance. Then, in a display of Flaubert's dialectical scepticism, he suddenly advances the arguments of Subjectivism: how can one be sure of any existence outside the perceiving self? Falling into the trap, Antoine naively responds: 'But you exist, I can feel you'. Only an accidental contact with his prayer beads saves the hermit. Not for the first time the outward symbols of belief, whether recalled deliberately or by chance, dispel the threat of damnation.

Weary now, Antoine monologues on earlier themes: boredom, unease, doubt – just the moment to be tempted by Death, equally ready to offer eternal nothingness or the hope of eternal joy. But Lust reappears to offer all the pleasures the ascetic has denied himself. Antoine interrupts their argument: perhaps beyond death lies more suffering and beneath lust 'an even gloomier nothingness, an even broader despair'. The Devil tries again, with a parade of Divinities from the earliest mythologies to the Bible and Rome. Each recounts its rise, fall and replacement by a successor destined to the same fate. The sheer variety of forms proves that the Divine is no more immutable than eternal. As Logic says: 'Since they have all passed, yours too . . . '. Yet Antoine defies the Devil, renouncing his quest for knowledge and praying for God's help to carry on. The Devil stays Death's hand, knowing he has not won Antoine's soul. In his final speech he sheds new light on the pattern and meaning of this sprawling, vividly-physical work, by pointing out that all the sins, the curses, the threats and visions Antoine has faced in this longest of nights are *within*, inescapable because part of his complex and contradictory humanity. For all its cast of thousands, the play is the drama of the individual conscience, that of a modern like Flaubert rather than a Father of the Early Church, for the outcome is inconclusive. Antoine still prays for faith and God's mercy, but the Devil scornfully promises to return, locking protagonist and reader in a pattern of endless repetition.

Few critics disagree with the negative judgement of the work's first audience, Bouilhet and du Camp; and within a few years Flaubert lucidly acknowledged two major weaknesses: he had too closely identified with Antoine and in his enthusiasm written hastily, without a clear plan (II, 362). From *Madame Bovary* on, he corrected both: personal or autobiographical elements, from idealised love to the thirst for knowledge, appear in a critical perspective, while as much time and energy is devoted to planning as to research or writing-up. The nature of the 1856 revisions admits other faults. The text was slashed by more than half, largely by systematic shortening of speeches, descriptions or scenes; for the 1849 version suffers from the Romantic disease of galloping verbosity, indulging in accumulation, repetition and illustrative imagery.

In trying to exemplify his earlier preference for the concrete 'poet', Flaubert drowns his essential points, as even a sympathetic commentator admits: 'The ideological cohesion is lost in the evocation of material and historical detail'.[10] The narrative cohesion is scarcely more satisfactory, with many features likely to puzzle or irritate the reader. Although perhaps justified by the final message of eternal repetition, an idea which haunted many nineteenth-century writers, the jerky and unprepared recurrence of similar scenes of physical and psychological temptations, especially involving sexual desires, perversions and taboos, is as distracting as the variations in the rôle of the Devil from episode to episode.[11] Antoine himself is alternately tempted hero and mere onlooker, and shows few signs of psychological or intellectual development; a weakness partly corrected in the later versions, where he reacts and intervenes more.

There are positive qualities, especially when one remembers the literary context. Flaubert is quite at home in a Romantic form which perplexes the modern reader, who has simplified out the great variety of 'genres' practised before 1850 to the three which produced the finest and most accessible works: lyric poetry, stageable costume drama and prose fiction. Though like many Romantics he seems to maintain only a tenuous grasp on the overall shape, he shows skill in handling component parts, such as Antoine's psychological monologues and philosophical dialogues, and in varying his effects. He alternates not only debate and spectacle but also the crowded stage and the tête à tête, allegorical and human interlocutors, the solemn and the grotesque. Backgrounds also vary, from historical precision to mythical fantasy or pure symbolism, though they have in common a tendency, which Flaubert never lost, to sate the reader with things, just as the action here swamps him in violence. Flaubert's aesthetic dissatisfaction with the present, his passion for history and mythology, his continuing determination to tackle the ultimate questions of life directly, make him as reluctant, in 1849, to be a novelist, much less a realist, as his earlier mouthpiece Jules. In this perspective the peculiar achievements of *Madame Bovary* are all the more astonishing.

3
Flaubert's Literary Ideas

In a century during which so many creative writers devoted so much time to literary theory, few thought so long or so deeply about Art, literature and their own works as Flaubert. Yet few if any published so little on these subjects. The Romantic assault on Classical aesthetics led to a proliferation of prefaces and manifestos, and succeeding generations followed suit in propounding the principles of their schools and movements. Flaubert found the publication of aesthetic principles by creative writers repugnant. He published only one short text, devoted (nominally at least) to an analysis of the ideas and poetry of his great friend Bouilhet.[12] His private correspondence, however, is full of general theorising, personal revelations about his own works and practical criticism. Though the source has all the disadvantages of such a medium, from fragmentation to obscurity and self-contradiction, they are partly off-set by a blazing sincerity not always manifest in writers' public utterances. Indeed Flaubert only rarely modifies his views to take account of his correspondent: even when addressing his mistress, his closest friends or writers he respects and admires, he pulls no punches. Furthermore, the intimate nature of a correspondence helps to set the literary ideas in the necessary context both of his character and of his general vision of the world.

Like all great artists, Flaubert was a bundle of contradictions, as painful for him to live with as they were fruitful as creative stimuli.

His vision of the world is characterised from his youth by a conflict between an optimistic sense of human potential and a pessimistic, even nihilistic perception of human achievement. The latter, at first sight, dominates his correspondence. He repeatedly illustrated his 'small faith in happiness' (I, 201) calling life 'hideous' (IV, 182) or flat and boring (II, 84), refusing to recognise anything good in it (II,

22

290). 'I detest life' he told Louise Colet (III, 344), and he wrote to his mother from the Middle East that travel develops the contempt one feels for humanity (II, 290). As early as his mid-teens he was tempted to adopt a fashionable Byronic attitude of mocking scorn (I, 29-30). By his mid-twenties, though the distance and detachment remained (after his illness he had even incorporated them into his lifestyle), the laughter had become ambiguous, even contradictory. He wrote of '*le grotesque triste*' (the sad grotesque), finding even within himself many aspects of 'this ridiculousness intrinsic in human life itself' I, 262), something akin to what the twentieth century would call the Absurd.

Unlike some modern exponents, however, he saw no way out, for together with his pessimistic disillusionment, a deep fatalistic determinism was one of the few philosophical principles he felt certain about (I, 319). On all the other main questions of existence, he subscribed to the scepticism of the great Renaissance Frenchmen Rabelais and Montaigne: we cannot know anything for certain, especially if gifted with the ability to see the antithesis, the other side, of each issue (I, 228). In his youth he found the uncertainty frightening and longed to achieve a simple unity (I, 60-1). But later he elevated it to a central principle: not to conclude (II, 239). A typical case was the argument matter v. spirit, which raged throughout the century. Unable to shake off either his instinctive feeling for the spiritual or his reasoned scientific materialism, he finally came to the conclusion, in his mid-forties, that:

. . . I don't know what the two nouns Matter and Spirit mean; we don't know one any more than the other. They are perhaps only two abstractions of our intelligence. In a word, I find Materialism and Spiritualism *two equal impertinences*. (V, 367).

His main objection to the mass of his contemporaries (scornfully called 'the bourgeois', the word having more the meaning of the English 'philistine' than any class-reference) was that they were always ready to draw facile conclusions.

Human potential, in contrast, was found either in the fragile qualities of dream and aspiration to something better than one knows, so easily crushed by reality; or more toughly and permanently in the concrete activity of the Artist. From his early teens he set Art above all other human endeavour. To a certain extent this

was because it offered an alluring flight from reality, especially
for the creator, free to choose, for a time, the world he inhabited
– a point he was still making in middle-age. But Art's main value
was as a carrier of truth about the real world and about humanity.
Influenced by the Platonic tradition, by French Classicism and by
the Romantic theory of the poet-as-prophet, he saw this truth as
a kind of absolute. Hence he castigated those whose art expressed
only the most narrowly-personal experience; he constantly reminded
them of the Olympian *impersonality* of the greatest writers, Homer or
Shakespeare.

Likewise he separated true Art from actuality. Commitment
to moral, social and political causes had become popular among
imaginative writers in France by 1840, but Flaubert always stood
aloof. Though he admired the distinguished historian and critic
Taine, he had reservations about his influential idea that a work
of art expresses a 'moment' in time and space:

> . . . a work has importance only by virtue of its eternity, that
> is to say the more it represents humanity as it has always been,
> the more it will be beautiful. The way to be ideal is to be true
> and that can only be achieved by choice and by exaggeration.
> All the difference consists in exaggerating harmoniously. (Sup.
> II, 118, 1867)

The last word is no less crucial for an understanding of Flaubert's
stance: beauty is as important as truth. Like Keats he repeatedly
links the two; and at times is tempted to put beauty first, especially
in his revulsion at the ugliness of modern life. Some of his contemporaries took this retreat into Beauty to extremes, propounding
a theory of Art for its own sake, the creation of gratuitous but
aesthetically satisfying objects. They laid great stress on formal
values and on craftsmanship: a welcome development after the
careless, often 'inspirational' attitude to composition adopted by
the Romantics. Flaubert shared this preoccupation, for he regretted
the lack of stylistic polish manifested by many major figures of the
century, both Romantic (from Larmartine to Hugo) and Realist (from
Balzac to Zola). But in his case form was never an end in itself. Style is
'an absolute way of seeing things' (II, 346), and, he insists, 'you can't
separate the form from the Idea, for the Idea exists only by virtue
of its form' (I,321). Although he once dreamt of composing 'a book

about nothing' (II, 345), it is difficult, in the context of his concept of style, to grasp what he meant. Certainly his books, from the earliest elucubrations to the mature novels, are all about something, indeed they tackle the great questions of human existence.

Turning from his broad generalities to his reflexions on his own writing, we find again the central contradiction between aspirations and banal reality. He admits to being, as a writer, equally fascinated by both:

> There are in me, on the literary plane, two distinct fellows: one who is fond of great cries, of lyricism, of eagle's flights, of all the sonorities of the sentence and the summits of philosophical thought (*l'idée*); another who quarries the real as much as he can, who likes to stress the little fact as much as the great one, who would like to make people feel almost physically the things he reproduces; this chap likes to laugh and is at home in Man's animalities. (II, 343-4, 1852)

He gives the impression, often, of exercising the 'two fellows' alternately, by his choice of contrasting themes, as in the passage from *Madame Bovary* to *Salammbô*. But his deepest tendency is to yoke them together, however risky the process. In the letter just quoted he goes on to say that the first *Education Sentimentale* had been such an attempt, but unsuccessful. A little later, he describes his aim in *Madame Bovary* thus:

> The whole value of my book, if it has a value, will be that it has managed to walk straight on a hairsbreadth tightrope over the double abyss of lyricism and vulgarity (which I want to blend together in a narrative analysis). (II, 372)

This coexistence of contradictory extremes serves at once his sceptical belief in 'antithesis', his sense of the 'sad grotesque' and his general refusal to conclude. It relates also perhaps to his conviction that the modern writer must be prepared to treat any subject, because 'each atom of matter contains some thought', ready to be extracted as 'poetry' (III, 138). The principle of impersonality emerges again, for it is not merely the ability to refrain from talking too much about oneself, but part of a whole strategy of writing, and a profoundly ambiguous one. In his early thirties, in reaction against personal emotion in Art, he is calling for the introduction of the cold scalpel of modern science; he also approves of the current scientific ideal of adding to knowledge bit by bit; not making sweeping claims, but, like Art, simply showing things as they are (Plé. II, 77). The role of the artist is to *represent*, he says repeatedly; let us be satisfied with *the picture*. His goal, it gradually emerges, is to produce a literary work which will have the same effect on the reader that reality itself has on him, Flaubert. When, in a famous letter, he compares the author to God, it is not so much a figure of speech as a logical consequence of this link:

> The author in his work must be like God in the Universe, everywhere present, nowhere visible. As Art is a second nature, the creator of that nature must operate similar processes. One must feel in every atom, in every aspect, a hidden, infinite impassibility. The effect, for the spectator, must be a kind of astonishment. How was all that made? he must say, and feel crushed without knowing why. (II, 61-2, 1852)

He is perfectly aware that the work is the creation of an individual mind, imbued with a particular vision; impersonal only in the second degree, in that the author nowhere draws attention to himself. In 1868 he clarified this point for his friend George Sand, a leading exponent of the committed literature of the time:

> . . . I don't think that I have the right to accuse anybody. I don't even believe that the novelist should express *his* opinion about the things in this world. He can communicate it, but I don't like him to say it. (That's part of my poetics.) (V, 396)

Earlier exponents of literature as scientific representation, notably Balzac, had assimilated the role of the novelist to that of the historian (the social scientist had not yet been invented). He would show all his evidence, add his analytical commentary and draw his conclusions. An obtrusive omniscient narrator was thus essential. With Flaubert, it is a case of the reluctant novelist of the 1840s turning at a stroke into the 'disappearing novelist' of his mature fiction. Once he abandoned the wide variety of Romantic literary forms for sober realism, his whole theory and practice was to be based merely on the 'showing'. The obtrusive narrator of his early works disappears, and much more attention is paid to concrete description of places, people and their actions. Of *Madame Bovary* he wrote: 'The reader won't notice, I hope, all the psychological work hidden under the form, but he'll feel its effect'. (IV, 3, 1854)

Yet his precepts, as he writes his first 'realistic' novel, continue to float ambiguously between scientific realism and an attitude almost Romantic, as in the final twist of this remark:

> What seems to me the highest point in Art (and the most difficult) is neither to make people laugh nor cry, neither to get them on heat nor in a rage, but to act on them as nature does, that is to say, to *make them dream*. (III, 322, 1853)

This is excellently glossed by Alison Fairlie:[13]

> The expression 'faire rêver' stands for two of his most deeply ingrained reactions: an intellectual sense of the contrasts, complexities and paradoxes that make it impossible to sum up human behaviour in facile categories of good and evil (. . .) and a kind of sheer marvelling stupefaction before the richness and strangeness of things as they are.

Similarly, the stress on impassibility does not imply coldness in the creator. He must detach himself from his own feelings the better to grasp those of others:

> The poet is now called upon to have sympathy for *everything* and for *everybody*, in order to understand and describe them. We lack science above all. (IV, 243, 1857)

At times he even prescribes a symbiotic relationship, perhaps inspired by the experience of pantheistic fusion with Nature he had known as a young man and described in his youthful writings. Hence his complex advice to Louise Colet:

> Let's always remember that impersonality is the sign of force. Let us absorb the objective, let it circulate in us, let it reproduce itself on the outside without anyone being able to understand anything about this marvellous chemistry. Our heart must be good only

for feeling that of others. Let's be magnifying mirrors of exterior reality. (III, 383-4, 1853)

An identification he several times reported enjoying himself; for example:

. . . it's a delightful thing to be writing, no longer to be oneself, but to circulate throughout the creation one is talking about. Today, for example both man and woman, lover and mistress at once, I took a horse ride in a forest one autumn afternoon, under yellow leaves, and I was the horses, the leaves, the wind, the words they said and the red sun that caused them to half-close their eyes, drowned in love. (III, 405, 1853)

But just as the intention to puzzle the reader remains constant, so the theme of irony is never far away when he discusses attitudes and tonalities. Only a few months after these letters, he describes the ideal of the modern writer as 'the ironic acceptance of existence and its plastic and complete remodelling by art' (IV, 15, 1854). Laughter, he says, is 'disdain and understanding mixed, the highest way of seeing life'(IV, 33); he talks of an attitude of a 'superior joke' (III, 37, 1852), and even of 'lyricism in jokiness' (II, 402, 1852). In 1846, while his own creative endeavours were coming to grips with the extravagant subject, and planning the no less extravagant form of his *La Tentation de Saint Antoine*, he had urged Louise Colet to write 'a big novel, very simple, a mixture of irony and feeling, that is to say, true' (I,370). She of course ignored his advice; but it stands as good a one-line assessment of *Madame Bovary* as any made during or after its composition. For the fusion of the lyrical and the vulgar clearly implied that of feeling and irony, not just for the author but also for the reader. While insisting that the first conversation between Emma and Léon (II, ii), full of poetic subjects, was intended to be grotesque (as indeed it is), he added, 'The irony takes nothing away from the pathos; on the contrary, it exaggerates it'. And went on, 'In my third part, which will be full of farcical things, I want to draw tears'. (III, 42-3, 1852)

There were other difficult, but potentially fruitful tensions to be faced by the practising novelist, for 'Science' could clash with 'Art' as well as with 'emotion'. Flaubert's obsession with accumulating the best and most complete documentation available, though partly attributable to an awareness of the limitations of his personal experience of the world, also springs from his worship of modern science with its determination to get the facts exactly right. Thus he would not even trust his memory when, by an unfortunate chance he found himself in Paris writing a description of Rouen Cathedral: he fired off a detailed questionnaire to a friend on the spot (Plé. II, 570-1). Scientific too, was his strict application of logic: to character-development, for example. Unscientific, in both these ways, seemed to be most of the new novels he read, to which he applied an increasingly precise and detailed practical criticism as he gained expertise in fiction-writing himself. But the document was never allowed to dominate aesthetic considerations, as it did with so many of his contemporaries and naïve imitators. He was as severe on failings of beauty as on those of truth. He had insisted since his mid-twenties that the work of Art, whatever its subject, must have unity and carefully-prepared overall shape (I, 375, 1846).

He now paid equal attention to the balancing of the components. The novelist had to have a painter's grasp of the relative importance of the parts, and know how to place them in the appropriate 'ground' (IV, 292, 1858). Of the three basic bricks of fiction – narrative, description, dialogue – he found it easiest to control the last: unlike most of the writers whom his correspondence analyses. He was often unhappy about the proper balance of the other two in his own works despite the painstaking planning which went into them. *Madame Bovary*, he thought, had too much preparation in relation to its action, while the later chapters of *Salammbô* had too much military action for the psychological content. He may have undertaken *Madame Bovary* to curb his lyrical tendencies, but certainly not to escape the need to write well. Rather, he saw the banal subject, commonplace characters and dull milieu as a challenge to be both true and beautiful (III, 338, 1853); and this applies particularly to style. His dream of modern literature achieving a prose as perfect as the best verse was, like the prescriptions of so many creative writers, only a generalised projection of his own practice, as he measured out *Madame Bovary's* progress in paragraphs per week.

While struggling to satisfy these contradictory demands, to fuse the two sides of his literary personality, Flaubert would occasionally seek release by entertaining fresh projects, exotic, lyrical or metaphysical, telling his friends that his modern novel, *Madame Bovary*,

was only a disciplinary exercise (IV, 134, 1856). In turning to the
subject of religions, love and war in ancient Carthage, he probably
saw the composition of *Salammbô* as relatively unproblematic; indeed
he briefly entertained the idea of writing it quickly, in a 'broad and
lively style' (IV, 209, 1857). Perhaps he remembered affectionately
the enthusiastic, even feverish, composition of *La Tentation*. And yet
before starting his Carthaginian novel, he had applied the principles
of scientific realism and Art-for-Art craftsmanship to a revision of
that sprawling drama. And within weeks of beginning the novel he
was 'worried . . . by the psychological element' (IV, 175), unable to
perceive the 'landscape' clearly or to 'feel' the religion (IV, 189).
Once he started writing chapter I, his prime concern was to 'make
people see' the city and the characters; and in a first version this goal
of representation clashed unhappily with the fictional techniques
employed (IV, 226-7).

Next he was lamenting that because he couldn't feel himself into
Carthaginian minds and hearts he couldn't express them (IV, 243).
Documentation piled up on his desk, as it had for the modern novel;
but only when he had been to the site of Carthage – though there was
little enough left to see – did he finally get under way. No imaginative
self-indulgences, then, but a dogged quest for 'reality' (IV, 345,
1859), even though he considered it 'almost impossible in such a
subject' (IV, 379, 1860). He was determined not to be 'pohetical'
(ib). Everything, finally, was researched and planned down to the
last detail, and scrupulously executed. Five more years of his life
were swallowed up.

Then on to the next novel and five more years of scholarship
and composition, living with, and constantly meditating on, the
conflicting demands of beauty and truth, irony and feeling. Ending
each time with a work which did not fully satisfy him, though
in the face of uncomprehending and often derogatory reviews
he was confident of some qualities. After eighteen years practising the craft of fiction, and three completed novels, he wrote
to George Sand (in forty-five years of writing she published over
fifty novels):

> Will I be able to write a book in which I will give all of myself? It
> seems to me, in moments of vanity, that I'm beginning to glimpse
> what a novel must be. But I still have three or four to write before
> that (which, besides, is pretty vague), and at the rate I'm going I'll

be lucky to write the three or four (. . .) I have contradictory *ideals*.
(IV, 2, 1869)

There was, alas, only one more novel to come. But the 'contradictory
ideals' had already produced a revolution in the way of thinking and
writing fiction.

4

Madame Bovary

The critical condemnation of *La Tentation* by his trusted friends paralysed Flaubert's creative processes for a year. Only in September 1850 did he begin to regain confidence. Bouilhet reminded him of an old project: a dictionary of bourgeois clichés and received ideas. He responded that it should have a preface so subtly ironic that the reader would be unsure whether the book contained valuable knowledge or a collection of stupidities (II, 237-8). But he soon turned to fiction, weighing up three possible ways of treating the theme of unsatisfiable desire: in Don Juan, in a woman longing to be loved by a God, in a modern Flemish girl whose quiet life hides inner turbulence and tortured mysticism.

Though pursuing the Don Juan project, he was convinced that he should be tackling a modern subject in a modern manner. On returning to France he seized upon the unhappy tale of Delamare, the 'health officer' of a village near Rouen, focussing mainly on his young second wife. However all the four earlier projects would reappear more or less distorted in his account of ordinary middle-class Normans facing everyday problems such as incompatibility in marriage, adultery and debt.

The whole enterprise seemed to him alien to a literary personality dominated by lyrical or satirical excess. He saw it as a valuable exercise in unfamiliar territory, with his own detachment helping the pursuit of his new literary goal of impersonality. He would give it the slow rhythm of life itself, not the paroxysms of drama. Although he admired theatrical form because 'it annuls the author' (III, 61), that author had been all too present in *La Tentation*. The new novel, while less obviously full of significant ideas than the 'play', would be subtly more daring, and have greater aesthetic artistry, without any sacrifice in documentary rigour. We saw in Chapter 3 how, to satisfy the contradictory impulses of his literary personality, he sought to fuse the gut creativity and philosophical aspirations of Romanticism, the craftsmanlike priorities of Art for Art and the documentary and scientific approach of the new Realists. Thus he could write both 'The artist must elevate everything' and 'I will have made a piece of written reality – and that is rare' (III, 249, 268). This balancing act allows the work, in effect, to rise above the limitations of each of the rival aesthetics. It has feeling and ideas, conscious artistry, and a high level both of specific verisimilitude and of general truth.

Even in *Madame Bovary*, detachment and concealment did not come easily, for Flaubert's views on modern France and everyday mediocrity were as forceful as those on religion or the aspirations of a Saint Antony. He kept their explicit expression for his correspondence, trying in the novel to achieve the impenetrable irony of the unwritten dictionary-preface. He knew the risks, as he observed of one of the speeches of Monsieur Homais, the village intellectual:

> I find it grotesque, but no doubt I'll be well and truly caught out over it, because the bourgeois will find it profoundly reasonable. (III, 184)

We saw earlier how the irony enveloped Emma and her lovers. Flaubert extended a compensatory sympathy to the husband who unwittingly causes much of her suffering. Indeed she herself frequently attracts the sympathetic epithet 'poor' in his letters; yet she is also shown as a speaker of clichés, a cardinal sin. Summing her up for his correspondents, he wrote of a 'female character naturally corrupt' (IV, 136) and 'a somewhat perverse nature, a woman of false poetry and false feeling' (IV, 168).

Critical evaluations of Emma over 130 years, compared with these remarks, suggest that Flaubert succeeded better than he intended in baffling and perplexing his readers, in setting them dreaming. In the year of publication his great contemporary Baudelaire saw her as a figure of heroic potential who has the misfortune to live in an unredeemably mediocre environment.[14] Others since have stressed her independence, her will and energy, her aspirations, her dissatisfaction with lower middle-class provincial life and with the inferior status accorded women, the last point being taken up in the title itself.

Balzac and Stendhal had painted galleries of heroic females, both in this active mould and in the more socially acceptable mould of noble self-abnegation. Flaubert's own early works had few female protagonists, one or two of whom displayed spirit or intelligence; but he had shown little inclination to give *any* protagonist unequivocal heroic status, whether measured in terms of energy, morality or intelligence.

The opening pages of *Madame Bovary* take things even further. Charles Bovary and his family are distinguished, if that is the right word, by their very ordinariness: their world consists of an accumulation of trivia. Any unusual features belong to the domain of the grotesque, not the noble. Charles as a schoolboy possesses a hat of stupefying oddity, his father is a middle-aged drop-out, his mother's aspirations for him are absurdly out of key with his modest potential. In earlier writers, the petty background would function as a contrast to protagonists of a different scale. Charles is no Julien Sorel, and Emma's principal distinction, at first, seems to be her physical charm. Temperamentally volatile and moody, restless in the isolated family farm, she longs for change, but her status and education have prepared her for only a modest upward social mobility. Her unrealistic and clichéd wish for a midnight wedding, while helping to set her apart, hardly inspires confidence in the nature and quality of her difference!

Charles is happy and fulfilled by Emma's mere presence, infinitely more attractive than that of his first wife. The modern reader, accustomed to contemporary frankness in sexual matters, must remember that though French writers of the nineteenth century enjoyed greater freedom than the English, there were limits, especially during the selective prudery of the Second Empire. Flaubert's letters and drafts show the importance he attached to sexuality in his characterisations, but with few exceptions his final text had to camouflage this element. He does indicate that Charles is sexually satisfied in the marriage, while Emma is not. Indeed in general she is puzzled by her new status, since feelings and experiences do not conform to those promised by her youthful reading. Unlike Flaubert, almost a born pessimist, Emma conceives adult life, love and marriage as offering endless joys, delights and excitements in exotic and luxurious settings. One might see this as supporting Baudelaire's argument that she is deformed progressively by surroundings from which, as a woman, she has little chance to escape; it is for this reason that she longs to have a son.

But the effect of adolescent reading is by no means the only theme
Flaubert treats in his flashback description of her youth and convent
education (I, vi). Her attitude to religion shows her to be shallow,
sensual and uncritical; confusing Catholicism with her adolescent
sexuality and sentimentality, she parodies the unwritten story about
the woman who loves a God. The death of her mother exposes her
as a selfish actress, coping with bereavement by transferring it to
the plane of her reading and going through the motions she thinks
appropriate to a heroine. The speed with which she loses interest in
this rôle, then in that of running her father's household, points to
innate restlessness and impatience. Emma will always be as easily
bored as captured by new stimuli. Throughout the chapter, Flaubert
insists on the interplay between her 'nature' or her 'temperament'
and her adolescent experiences. Analytical remarks cut through to
the basic essence. She has all the selfish pragmatism and materialism
an urban intellectual might attribute to peasant stock:

> She had to be able to draw from things a personal profit, and
> she rejected as useless anything that did not contribute to the
> immediate needs of her heart. (I,vi)

Her reported thoughts, like her actions, display neither intelligence nor self-awareness; and this limits the value of her real
qualities, such as the concrete, intensely-visual imagination she
shares with her creator. Though she is a prey to secret longings
and aspirations, recalling the Flemish mystic imagined in 1850, they
have in her no genuine religious or metaphysical dimension. The
novelist, while eschewing explicit commentary, deploys a range of
strategies that invite at least a provisional evaluation. We see the
poor impression she makes on her teachers, and some illustrative
images are negatively charged:

> (she) dirtied her hands with the dust from old circulating libraries
> (. . .)

After a list of the mediocre pictures which excited her, the narrator
forgets himself so far as to launch a mock-heroic address:

> You too were there, sultans with long pipes (. . .)

One is forced to agree with Margaret Tillett:[15]

> . . . if she had all the good fortune in the world, second-rate
> as a human being she would be condemned to remain.

Flaubert's psychology, though by no means simplistic (there are
many more nuances in this single chapter) is at once essentialist
and logical. Characters form and transform, but only within the
limits laid down by their 'temperament'.

Emma married cannot escape her limitations. Charles' satisfaction
with his modest lifestyle and happiness spells incompatibility, but
the blame is shared, since she fails to grasp his down-to-earth
qualities and misses the depth of his affection. This failure sig-
nals another cardinal sin, for Flaubert. As the terse analysis puts
it, she is:

> . . . incapable of understanding anything she did not experience,
> or of believing in anything that did not present itself in conven-
> tional forms. (I,vii)

Received ideas inhibit self-awareness in Emma, as in almost every
character in the novel. She wrongly, persistently and in the end
fatally sees herself as a heroine. Received ideas also prevent her from
seeing the rest of the world clearly. Flaubert went to great lengths
to describe the world around his characters. Early critics found
much of this gratuitous, perhaps because it lacked the elucidatory
commentary of the no less descriptive Balzac. Some description,
as more recent critics have seen, is mediated by a character, and
hence serves as indirect psychological portrayal. But elsewhere the
point is precisely in the description's independence of the clichéd
or blinkered perception of the characters or of their unrealistic
dreams. Indeed, many of Emma's dreams will be punctured by
an intervention from this 'real' world.

The clash between reality and Emma's perceptions becomes
more complex when the couple are offered a close-up of aristocratic
luxury by a chance invitation to a ball at a local stately home, La
Vaubyessard. This brief visit is recounted at great length, to mark
out its importance. It confirms, for Emma, the authenticity of the
image of reality presented by her reading. She sees a man who slept
with Marie Antoinette, and a love-letter change hands, she hears of

travel to exotic lands, she dances with an aristocrat. Throughout she bathes in the physical pleasures offered by luxury and elegance. This gives her dreams a new impetus and a new shape. They focus on a vaguely perceived Paris, and require a physical prolongation, for the analysis explains:

> In her desire she confused the sensualities of luxury with the joys of the heart, the elegance of habits with the delicacies of feeling. (I, ix)

The confusion of luxury and love, once installed, will drive Emma inexorably to despair and debt, to emotional and literal bankruptcy. The early effects, though, are mild: she buys pretentious little luxuries for the home, feels frustrated at Charles' modest success (the 'health officer' is markedly inferior to the qualified doctor and practises in small communities).

A year later disappointed hope for another invitation precipitates a nervous crisis and depression. The doctor's son-turned-novelist pushes characterisation to new extremes of realism, clinically exposing the relation between mind and body as Emma's complex frustrations manifest themselves physically and psychologically. The nature and form of his implicit diagnosis are strikingly modern – too much so for the fictional medical men, who apply old-fashioned remedies: a change of air and of scene.

With the move to Yonville, another isolated, rather backward community, the novel opens up beyond the confines of the Bovary and Rouault families to offer a miniature portrait gallery of middle-class village types. An inn-keeper, a chemist, a tax collector, a shopkeeper, the parish priest, a notary and his young clerk are vividly drawn in appearance, gesture and word. In Léon, the clerk, Emma finds a kindred spirit with whom to exchange Romantic clichés, though his taste is notably softer and more moderate than hers, prefiguring a reversal of sex-stereotypes in their relationship. Having demolished – however discreetly – Emma's pretensions to superiority via her imagination and her aspirations (both tainted at source), Flaubert begins to offer hints that her real superiority may be found elsewhere. From the beginning of her relationship with Léon a 'reciprocal sympathy' (II,ii) flows beneath the clichés. It grows in intensity and complexity, taking on erotic undertones in Emma, while Léon's timidity sublimates it into harmless contemplation.

Emma's health is again threatened, and she unsuccessfully tries to treat her problem with religion, the priest proving as obtuse as the doctors. When Léon leaves to continue his studies, the parting is charged with intense but unspoken emotion, communicated to the reader by images for once devoid of ironic deflation:

> They looked at each other; and their thoughts, merging in the same anguish, clung tightly to each other, like breast beating against breast.

They shake hands:

> Léon felt (her hand) between his fingers and the very substance of his whole being seemed to him to descend into that damp palm. (II, vi)

Emma is plunged again into suffering and despair verging on the pathological. Flaubert ironically has Charles and his mother attribute this to her current reading habits. They are some ten years too late, for Emma's condition is now the product of the negative configuration of her real experiences when compared to deeprooted expectations born of her teenage reading.

Her next key experience reveals its negative configuration to the reader from the start. Rodolphe Boulanger, a local landowner, is shown to be a coarse provincial Don Juan attracted only by Emma's physical charms. Blinded by her ideal and limited in her understanding of other people, she, however, is taken in. The celebrated 'symphonic' description of the agricultural show (II, viii), unlike the earlier wedding chapter (I, iv) which sacrificed the psychological to the social, keeps a careful balance. A battery of juxtaposition techniques uses the public events to point up the shallowness and gullibility at work in the relationship between Emma and Rodolphe. Yet all is not negative, for the scene is also an intense, crypto-erotic experience culminating in an almost orgasmic handclasp. As in the farewell scene with Léon, both partners are caught up in the emotion:

> They looked at each other. A supreme desire made their dry lips tremble, and loosely, without effort, their fingers merged. (II, viii)

*

Even Rodolphe, thus moved, can dream of an endless perspective of days of love. Incidentally, for all Rodolphe's crude but effective seduction techniques, the key to Emma's metaphorical surrender lies in a spontaneous sense-triggered memory of past moments of delight. First Rodolphe's hair-oil recalls that of her partner at La Vaubyessard, then the sight of the Rouen coach reawakens the emotions experienced with Léon. The role of involuntary memory, almost a discovery of Romantic writers and taken to its culmination in Marcel Proust (whose narrator retrieves the central experiences of his childhood from the taste of a sponge cake dipped in tea), is important throughout the novel, serving as a touchstone for the positive qualities of the characters, as measured by their depth of feeling. Later, Rodolphe, attempting to recall past loves from the souvenirs he has kept, is thwarted as much by his own shallowness as by the conscious effort to recall: like Proust, Flaubert insisted that the trigger must be met accidentally, not sought.

The relationship with Rodolphe soon becomes adulterous. There is erotic satisfaction at first, but Emma's playacting takes the edge off the spontaneity which has encouraged Rodolphe to treat her less cynically than usual. She in her turn comes to feel subjugated rather than elevated. Another vivid memory, of her youth and innocence at home before her marriage, emphasises how her life has been a sequence of lost illusions insidious in their effect (II, x). She tries to turn Charles into a glamorous hero by encouraging him to perform an operation on the village cripple. Her heartless response to his failure illuminates her selfishness (II, xi); as does her general attitude to her daughter, born soon after the arrival in Yonville.

She throws herself back into the liaison with Rodolphe, desperately dressing it in luxury items purchased from the rather too aptly named M. Lheureux (the lucky, or happy, one). Yet lest the reader by lulled by this materialism into a simplifying judgement on Emma, Flaubert returns again to the theme of her authenticity of feeling, making the longest and most personal of his rare authorial intrusions. He openly castigates Rodolphe for his inability to recognise, behind Emma's banal language, the reality and intensity of her emotions. As a writer he shares, every day, her communication problem, and by the end of the intervention the fictional pretext has given way to the novelist's own cry, which has rarely been so economically, yet forcefully, expressed:

> ... no-one, ever, can give the precise measure of his needs, his ideas, his sufferings, and (...) human language is like a cracked pan on which we beat out melodies that would make a bear dance, when we really want to soften the heart of the stars. (II, xii)

The unexpected complicity of the narrator finds a new expression in the lovers' final meeting, when Emma is convinced they are about to flee together. Even the calculating Rodolphe, who has no intention of going through with the plan, is caught up in an atmosphere of joy, harmony and peace which Nature all around seems to echo. Flaubert's customary insistence on the magisterial indifference of Nature to Man's moods is for once abandoned in favour of the Romantic device of pathetic fallacy. But Rodolphe's superficiality makes it easy for him, once alone, to break the spell and compile a hypocritical letter of farewell. The reader appreciates here, as with other emotionally shallow characters, Lheureux or Homais, the obverse side to the theme of communication. Such people have no difficulty in using language because they are not caught in the trap of feeling like Emma, or seeking an absolute truth like Flaubert; they need words only to set bears dancing.

Emma will not dance to the tune of Rodolphe's letter. She has once again been frustrated, and the collapse is proportional to the expectation thwarted. It is not surprising that she even briefly envisages suicide as the pain is intensified by a too-faithful memory flashing up images of past happiness. There follows a long period of physical and psychological illness, tended by the devoted if uncomprehending Charles. Another type of discourse is juxtaposed here, that of M. Homais, the chemist, in his confident scientific explanations. It is easy to see the grotesque elements, especially as Flaubert shows an unusual indulgence towards his garrulity. Yet his words contain a real element of truth, as when he suggests that Emma is unusually sensitive; and even his suspicions of an allergy to apricots half-grasp the way her disturbed mind and body react to all the objects which hold and trigger painful memories for her.

She emerges from her long convalescence profoundly marked by the relationship with Rodolphe. She unconsciously stores her memories. Nearer consciousness is the deprivation caused by the removal of a satisfying sexual relationship. On the conscious level her habit of adultery has given her more confidence, less gullibility in her relations with men. For a time, though, her illness leaves her in a state of passivity, an abdication of the will. She seeks religious consolation again, unsuccessfully. A visit to the Opera at Rouen revives old dreams of adventure and aristocratic luxury, her faculty for identification with a fiction being taken to new extremes as she loses herself in the dramatic experience, longing to be carried off by the opera's hero. She is emotionally prepared to exploit a chance meeting with Léon; and, helped once more by vivid memories, she is drawn into a new adultery. The narrator is careful to show how, though based on genuine attraction, the relationship is also built on lies, for Emma is desperate to find a life-enhancing experience and Léon, less timid after his years in the city, anxious to have a mistress. She succumbs in a closed cab, aimlessly criss-crossing the city: symbolic prefiguration of the atmosphere of constraint, secrecy and claustration in which the whole affair will be conducted, in sharp contrast to the freshness of nature which framed her first adultery.

Distorted echoes are another structural feature of this episode. Emma at last has her longed-for 'honeymoon', but it is no more remote and exotic than the quiet riverside corners of Rouen; and the narrator is openly ironic about the couple's poeticisation of their surroundings (III, iii). On Emma's side there is calculation, desperation and self-deception as she pretends she has more than just a physical relationship. The self-deception grows more difficult to sustain when the initial intensity wears off. Emma is 'drying up all delight by wanting it too big'; and before long 'they knew each other too well to have those astonishments brought on by passion, which multiply a hundred fold its joy' (III, vi). Memories or dreams take Emma out of the disappointing present without bringing relief, since they offer a correcting perspective on what her liaison is. Thus a mediocre masked ball cruelly parodies La Vaubyessard. There are few signs in these chapters of the will-power and controlled energy praised by some readers in their heroine; but plenty of illustrations of her weaknesses, inadequacies and selfishness.

A host of practical pressures are also brought to bear, fruits of her compulsive spending and borrowing, for she is no more competent at handling the reality of money. Soon there are fresh signs of nervous disorder, worrying and puzzling Charles. Gradually the narration is preparing her final breakdown. Some critics have found her suicide inadequately motivated, usually because they are seeking a single clear-cut cause. As always, Flaubert is convincing by his very refusal to simplify. When Lheureux forecloses on her debts, Emma is already disappointed with Léon and disgusted with herself. There is no way of hiding the financial crisis from Charles; the public shame must be faced, unless she can find money quickly. Each refusal to help increases her desperation and brings out more of the unpleasant sides of her character.

She falls into facile role-playing, and her projection of herself as a heroine of fiction will influence her dramatic choice of escape-route. Léon's failure to help is just another setback, putting her attitude to their relationship in perspective. The appeal to Rodolphe is crucial, involving her most intense dreams and memories. Her angry reaction to his refusal reflects the irretrievable collapse of one more illusion: that the affair with him had been a real, superior form of love. As she leaves, the narrator insists that 'she was suffering only from her love' (III, viii). Reasoning is blotted out but not decision-making. The earlier temptation to suicide had taken a passive form – she could let herself fall from a window – because her mood was passive. This time the bold choice – to steal Homais' poison – fits her mood of febrile activity. Yet there is self-conscious role-playing. The 'transport of heroism' which initiates the act and the 'serenity of a duty accomplished' which she then feels, are surely her received ideas; as also the gesture of writing a note (with poor Charles as audience), and giving him instructions 'in a solemn voice'. The arsenic, though, will brook no play-acting, and the narration pitilessly unrolls the sequence of symptoms, overturning the centuries-old literary convention of the beautiful death.

Emma seems about to escape sharing the reader's awareness of ugliness, as a last gaze in the mirror coincides with a respite in the pain. But the voice of a blind beggar, a familiar figure on the road to Rouen during her affair with Léon, offers the ironic counterpoint of his song of young love, which Emma knows to be girlish illusion. Her bitter final laugh, though, seems to relate to a visual image as, 'thinking she could see the hideous face of the wretch', she dies in a moment of awareness of the ugliness of reality.

The unconventional, mould-breaking nature of Flaubert's narrative is underlined as it continues, in equally painstaking detail, through to Emma's burial and beyond. Life goes on for Yonville and for Charles; though he, at first transformed by her death then undermined by discovering the truth about her double life, does not long survive her. Homais' characteristic interference in insisting on a post mortem establishes there was no foul play. It is easy to forget, in the welter of precise details and the surrounding provincialities, that Flaubert here slips his readers a Romantic cliché even more elementary than the suicide of despair: the broken heart. However much he castigated clichés, Flaubert did not deny that many of them correspond with reality. The important thing was to see how much more complex that reality was.

Charles' death is also that of a pathetically broken mediocrity, not a hero. The successful characters in the novel similarly at once incarnate and parody clichés. Léon marries well, Lheureux's business expands, Homais flourishes professionally and politically. But these are successes on the scale of provincial life, not of traditional fiction, nor even of that consummate exaggerator of ordinariness, Balzac, who would not have settled for less than a million profit for each 'victor'. The modest scale established by Flaubert's opening pages remains firmly in place. The novelist may have technically 'disappeared', to leave us with a 'picture', but the very choice of elements points to a view of man contained in the twin themes of universal mediocrity and inevitable disillusion and defeat for all but a few.

Distinguished novelist-critics of the Anglo-Saxon tradition, which has always shown more concern than the French for the elevating role of the genre, have regretted the mature Flaubert's resolute choice of mediocre characters (or worse). But a Henry James or a D. H. Lawrence have tended to ignore the fact that their own protagonists are shaped by their personal vision and scale of values.[16] In any case the contradictory impulses in Flaubert ensure that some correcting perspective is offered. Three elements in particular seem to oppose the general image of human inadequacies. Two are minor characters, the third the narratorial presence itself.

Justin, Homais' poor relation and skivvy, and the eminent Dr Larivière, have in common only that they are at opposite ends of the medical hierarchy; and that they represent equally widely separated human qualities. Discreetly ever-present in Emma's entourage, Justin worships silently without ever trying to press his suit or actualise his love; hence he is spared disillusionment, if not pain. His is the innocent wonder of youth, and he escapes narratorial irony and sarcasm, though of course his life comes to no material success – he ends up a grocer's assistant in Rouen. Larivière too almost escapes narratorial irony. Modelled on Flaubert's father, he also incarnates in disguised form the qualities of Flaubert's ideal novelist. Possessing an eye which penetrates to the depths in diagnosis, a passionate devotion to his art and hands ready to plunge into wretchedness and suffering, he is contemptuous of public acclaim, practises a virtue he doesn't believe in and pities those in pain while remaining capable of cutting sarcasm. Yet he has a weak spot: a professional pride which makes him self-defensively slip out of the Bovary house while Emma is still alive, anxious not to have her die on his hands. The tiny detail is a typical manifestation of the superiority of the third positive presence: that of the novelist/contriver or narrator/observer of just such a revealing moment.

Modern criticism, reflecting twentieth-century trends in fiction as well as in critical theory, writes of 'implied authors' or 'the autonomous text'. The view is anachronistic for most nineteenth-century novelists, who saw no real break in continuity between themselves and the narratorial voice and stance in their fiction. In Balzac, in Stendhal, the narrator openly communicates the wisdom of the author. Flaubert's aim was to do it more subtly. He does not achieve total silence, intervening sometimes openly, as we have seen, more often indirectly, to compensate for the inadequacies of his characters. The narrator who makes us see, feel and understand Emma and the others represents a higher form of humanity than them, even than Larivière.

By refusing to make it easy for his readers, by demanding a level of concentrated attention to the texts which had hitherto been the preserve of the much shorter 'noble' forms of classical literature such as theatre or lyrical poetry, this narrator – honest, discreet, teasing the reader into patience and perspicacity but also into emotional identification – holds out just as much hope for the future of humanity as Flaubert himself, in his correspondence. Having criticised Baudelaire's view of Emma for its short-comings, it is only fair to acknowledge the accuracy of his overall assessment of the novel:[17]

This essentially suggestive book could prompt a volume of observations.

Suggestive, prompt (*souffler*), observations: Baudelaire's words are strikingly close to those used by Flaubert himself, and point to what Alison Fairlie has called 'the art of insinuation'. How do the novel's techniques carry this through?

We have already seen that the narrator was not always invisible. Indeed in the opening pages he is personalised as a fellow-pupil of Charles; and thereafter Flaubert exploits the useful and often untranslatable '*on*' (a form of the passive, an indefinite collective, but also, and increasingly since Flaubert's time, a colloquial equivalent of '*nous*'), to hint at a continuing presence as part of the milieu being described; so that one critic has written persuasively of an intermittent bourgeois narrator, complete with limited viewpoint and philistine values.[18] Elsewhere, in the presentation of Yonville most noticeably, he pastiches the expository school teacher tones of Balzac, though he still avoids Balzac's tendency to explain at length the significance of each object he describes. He has no modern qualms about offering a cutting analytical summary of character-traits or motives; and occasionally even proposes a generalisation or a maxim.[19] More discreetly, he uses figurative language both to deflate or criticise and to reinforce or intensify experiences described. On the whole he mostly tries to show, not to tell, offering a wealth of descriptions of everything from states of mind to landscapes. Here too his techniques are pragmatic, not dogmatic. Some descriptions invite the reader's evaluation by the nature and accumulation of chosen details, especially in the domain of the grotesque, as for example the wedding-feast and its centrepiece (I, iv). Others are more openly tendentious, making the significance explicit. Charles' hat, apart from its physical details, is 'one of those poor things whose silent ugliness has depths of expression, like the face of an idiot' (I, i); the portrait of the old servant Catherine Leroux ends: 'thus stood, before these bourgeois in full bloom, this half-century of servitude' (II, viii). Some passages present an 'omniscient narrator's viewpoint' of the objective reality around the characters, of which they may be oblivious; while others have a subjective slant, revealing the viewpoint and state of mind of a protagonist who is understood to be doing the looking: usually Emma, but quite often a male character contemplating her. Particularly striking are occasional passages, derived perhaps from Flaubert's own epileptic attacks, describing the hallucinatory distortions of reality which Emma perceives during her crises (II, xiii, III, viii).

Flaubert exploits the advantage his narrative stance offers over that of earlier or more recent novelists of the subjective perception. He is not tied to a realistic approximation of the perceiving and recording skills of the characters, which would be extremely limiting in his case. But unlike earlier novelists, he does not always spell out the presence or absence of character viewpoint, nor the shifts from one to another, leaving much 'decoding' to be done by the perceiving, or at least the perceptive, reader. Close examination reveals an astonishingly fluid and controlled modulation of point of view; so that the relatively static impression given by the novel's combination of substantial descriptions with a plot low on striking events or evident linear progression to a goal is compensated by the ceaseless movement of the reader within the 'pictures' Flaubert so lovingly sets up. The interiorisation of movements, together with the underlying principle of the relativity of viewpoint, is one of Flaubert's major legacies to later writers.

The mental landscapes, the characters' inner world, also exercised Flaubert's technical ingenuity. Though he subscribed to contemporary views of the importance of physiological factors in human character and conduct, he did not reduce people to mere impulses and stimulus responses. But as we have seen, the more subtle and sensitive protagonists are also the least competent at communication, or even self-analysis. Dialogue and theatre style monologue, favoured techniques of his great predecessors, are thus of limited value if form is accurately to reflect content. Flaubert chooses a mixture of narratorial analysis and unspoken inner monologue, the latter mostly through the 'dual voice' of a peculiar kind of 'reported speech' which offers the thoughts and words of the characters, unannounced and in the third person, thus blending them into the narrative.[20]

Often the thoughts and feelings, especially of Emma, defy even this discreet level of verbalisation, and he has recourse to the poetic techniques of imagery, seeking 'objective correlatives', as T. S. Eliot would call them. One of his similes lasts two whole paragraphs (II, vii). The novel also contains examples of a more directly mimetic rendering of the thoughts of the inarticulate, notably of Emma's father. But Flaubert's pioneering realism is, compared with the numerous vernacularist novelists of later generations (from the Zola of *L'Assommoir* to Céline, Queneau and even 'San-Antonio'), inhibited by his own double passion for clarity and beauty. The same inhibition, of course, affects his use of direct speech. When it is allowed to flow, it rings true in a way not found in the hyper-literary dialogues of his earlier fiction; a spin-off, no doubt, from his projected dictionary of clichés. But with the striking exception of Homais – who talks like a book anyway, albeit an encyclopaedia – direct speech is limited, partly to give the maximum relief to its important effects, partly to control the unavoidable vulgarity imposed by the choice of character, theme and milieu on a writer of great aesthetic sensibility.

The difficulties of 'writing vulgarity well' (III, 338) presented themselves everywhere. In descriptions, Flaubert's concern for rhythm and euphony joins his pursuit of the best expression to create aesthetically satisfying prose, even though the subject may be of little significance: the light effect on kitchen utensils, for example (I,iii). Flaubert had a painter's eye for effects of light and shade, like the Dutch masters with whom he is often compared for his general ability to transform banal subjects. Like them, too, he knew how to invest the everyday with a discreet symbolic weight, though his code, unlike theirs, is a private one, opening much of his texts to a plurality of readings.

The blind man is, to modern readers, an almost too obvious 'realisation' of the running theme of blindness in all the major characters. But he also represents a walking condemnation of specific weaknesses in individuals. Homais has failed to cure him and guiltily persecutes him to get him removed from the locality. As for Emma, some readers see him as a symbol of her guilt; while others, the present writer included, having difficulty in finding any traditional sense of sin in her, prefer to stress the way his ugliness opposes and finally neutralises Emma's desire to beautify the world and human experience (especially love, the theme of his song). Yet not only does Flaubert refuse to spell out the symbolic role, he also gives the man himself a vividly-realised physical presence, an excellent example of his compulsion to make his readers feel almost materially his chosen subjects.

The interaction of the concrete and the abstract, the specific and the general, the petty and the significant, can be seen in many aspects of the novel. Like the episodic blind man, the important secondary characters have symbolic functions as well as a concrete existence. In their case, though, it is a question of broadening the thematics of the novel, so that despite its parochial setting, cast and plot, *Madame Bovary* emerges as rather less of a 'scaling down' of Flaubert's ambition since the 1840s than it first seemed. Homais spells out his own representativity: not only the rational and anti-clerical Enlightenment, but also contemporary scientific positivism, figure in his running battle with the parish priest Bournisien, who though well-meaning and kindly, is devoid both of spirituality and intelligence, a fair reflexion, in Flaubert's view, of contemporary Catholicism. Rouen Cathedral is already largely a tourist attraction (III, i). Not that this assures the superiority of Homais' secular values, for the two fight their Lilliputian battle, across the corpse of Emma, to a draw, and finally doze off, 'after so much disagreement meeting at last in the same human weakness' (III, ix).

The authentic scientific attitude which Flaubert's correspondence frequently presented as the only hope for human progress, is represented by Dr Larivière, and hence comes off rather better in the world of the fiction, than Flaubert's beloved theme of Art. None of the characters has a proper appreciation of Art, being either closed to it like Charles, or superficial and uncritical like Emma. Those who practice it do so in ways which reflect Flaubert's own pet hates. Léon is an occasional dabbler, looking forward to the dilettantisms of Frédéric Moreau. The silent and unsociable Binet is a compulsive amateur woodturner, filling his house with useless objects; a parody of the Art-for-Art ideal of the self-absorbed craftsman, and a timely reminder that for Flaubert Art should never be gratuitous, but must have both meaning and value (III, vii). The only writer in the book is Homais, who in his aspirations to being a universal man engages in journalism and compiles scientific brochures for the sole purpose of self-promotion. He represents the pen at its most exploitative, least artistic and least true, to judge by his report of the agricultural show or his vitriotic 'news items' aimed against the blind man (III, xi).

Though constantly railing at the mercenary mercantilism of his age, Flaubert did not share some French novelists' passion for the theme of money itself. It plays a major role in Emma's downfall, with motifs like greed, overspending, debt and bankruptcy precisely paralleling developments in her emotional life; and the theme was scrupulously documented with the help of friends in law or business. But it never seems to spring off the page with quite the same vigour as the novel's many other themes. M. Lheureux, its main symbol, though offering a useful reminder that 'in-house credit' at inflated interest is not an invention of the card-carrying 1980s, seems to spark his creator's interest mainly in his role as a purveyor of examples of the bad taste and material clutter of bourgeois life (II, v, xii), and the means by which he gets rich at Emma's expense remain unclear.

Indeed, whereas Balzac created a whole range of money-maniacs as picturesque and imaginative as any other class of his characters, Flaubert's shopkeeper-financier is the least 'human' or 'rounded' figure in the novel, with none of the quirks of temperament, feeling or imagination which enliven Homais, Binet or Bournisien. Although this could be interpreted in Flaubert's favour as an early perception of the 'dehumanisation' process which Marx was to attribute to the practice of capitalism, Marx was no novelist, while Flaubert's aim was to give all his characters 'life'. The openly symbolic, if neatly ironical, surname chosen for the character suggests that Flaubert was quite aware of the problem.

The failure with Lheureux can probably be attributed to the fact that at this time Flaubert had no direct experience of the earning process and its importance in most people's lives. In this perspective it sheds light on the most famous, if least well documented, of his remarks about the novel: '*Madame Bovary, c'est moi*'. Most of the comments in his letters claim exactly the opposite: 'nothing in this book is taken from me'(III, 155), 'nothing that I like is in it' (IV, 134), and so on. Yet he admitted that the psychology of love it expressed was based – painfully at times – on his own experience, adapted, as he put it, to a bourgeois scale, 'to make it more general and human' (II, 457). Seeing himself ever as a monster, an exception, he would always make this particular modification in using his own experience, so that in a sense both extreme claims are correct: there *is* nothing of himself directly portrayed, certainly nothing of the artist, yet there is so much of the general humanity of Flaubert, scaled down to ordinariness, in the work. At all events, to call the novel 'a biography' (III, 247) was doubly modest: because he has created a gallery of fascinating characters, not just one, and because he has done so much more, in using them and their milieu to illustrate and question a wide range of themes of both contemporary and permanent interest. *Madame Bovary* is perhaps best perceived as a meditation on mediocrity magisterially disguised as a psychological novel.

5
Salammbô

In the spring of 1857 Flaubert's wide and eclectic knowledge of the history and religions of the southern Mediterranean, acquired for the composition of *La Tentation de Saint Antoine*, threw up another promising subject: the history of Carthage. Neglecting the best-known events, he fixed on an obscure period of three years (241-238 B.C.) when, defeated by Rome in the first Punic War, Carthage engaged in an increasingly vicious local conflict with its own mercenary army, which it had refused to pay off. Flaubert added two other themes: the documented description of the city and its civilisation, and a fictional story of the desperate passion of a mercenary leader for Salammbô, the daughter of the city's military and naval chief, Hamilcar. If the contrast with the petty provinciality of *Madame Bovary* offered scope to his love of grandeur, exoticism, poetic lyricism and the summits of philosophical thought, the choice of subject posed a new set of challenging problems.

Carthage was as badly-documented as it was little-known to the cultivated reader. Razed by Rome in 146 B.C., it had left no literature and few artefacts or architectural remains. This state of affairs was ideal for the superficial historical romancer, but Flaubert was incapable by now of writing that way. As we saw in Chapter 3, he intended to bring to the historical novel all the painstaking precision he had applied to the study of contemporary middle-class life. Thus for a few pages on commerce he read fifty volumes, making educated guesses from documents on contemporary cities and civilisations whenever necessary facts about Carthage were lacking. Yet he insisted on the need to fuse scientific methods with artistic and technical preoccupations. His Platonic view of form continued to link Truth closely to Beauty and aesthetic and stylistic perfection; while his psychology retained a classical orientation in its stress on the need to elevate individuals into types: 'paint what doesn't disappear, try to write for eternity' (IV, 425). Although *La Tentation* had again been shelved, the preoccupation with religion carried over into the new work. Though deeply sceptical, he was unwilling to reject metaphysics altogether. He urged a troubled correspondent to cease trying to reconcile religion and philosophy, and hang on to the values of science: 'Love facts for themselves. Study ideas as naturalists study flies'. (IV, 399)

When *Salammbô* was almost complete, he wrote:

The only thing to emerge from this book is an immense disdain for humanity. (IV, 445)

Scepticism, scientific detachment opening onto disdain for humanity: the thematic continuity with the Flaubert of *Madame Bovary* emerges clearly from the Correspondence. Yet at first the reader of the novel is struck by the contrasts and discontinuities. The setting is remote and exotic, the action vivid, violent and spectacular, and the stakes are high – from a rich city to divine knowledge. The protagonists are powerful figures both by their status and their human qualities, and the crowds they dominate play a major role throughout. Whereas the earlier novel takes place on the margin of history, *Salammbô* is set in the eye of a great storm. Not only climates and landscapes, but the civilisations they have bred, contrast sharply with the sleepy moderation of Normandy; as with each other, for Flaubert juxtaposes a wide variety of races, insisting on their diversity at all levels from costume to beliefs.

The role of religion is a further contrast. Despite Emma's intermittent religiosity, mid-nineteenth century France is portrayed as a secular, materially-orientated society, Catholicism being a part of social manners rather than a life-shaping force. In Carthage, the Gods play an important part in both individual and collective life. Religion is indeed just one of many themes which Flaubert uses to lock together the three centres of interest of the novel. However tightly locked they may be, it is necessary to separate them for the purposes of this brief account.

The war is the element most fully rooted in fact. Flaubert found the outline in twenty-three short chapters of the Greek historian Polybius' History, a near-contemporary record. He added a rich and colourful array of military detail from the great Greek and Roman literature of battle and siege, both historical and epic. His keynote was perhaps Polybius' summing-up: 'the most frightful and impious war I have ever heard of '. From the start the atmosphere is one of violence fuelled by mercenary resentment and Carthaginian fear. The mercenary army, raised to fight Rome, has been pulled back to Carthage after a peace settlement, but the city fathers are refusing to pay it off. Although it has a just grievance, it acts with indiscriminate violence during a celebration feast. Its fury is of short duration and it allows itself peacefully to be persuaded to move some distance away while the necessary payment is being raised.

Carthaginian violence, as manifested in the slaughter of a troop of mercenaries accidentally left behind, is colder and more deliberate. This episode, by the numbers involved, sets the curve of destruction on an upward movement which will continue, to culminate in mass annihilations of thousands of fighting men in the final phases of the war. (There were, of course, only six deaths in *Madame Bovary*!) The war theme is not merely an excuse for shock and horror (though there is plenty of both, in often disturbing reminders that one of Flaubert's favourite authors was the Marquis de Sade). Flaubert offers in dramatised, fiction form, an interpretation of warfare as well as a concrete portrayal of its Classical manifestations from individual combat through skirmish, surprise attack, unprepared confrontation, ambush and siege to the formally-agreed and mathematically-prepared battle on an open field. He shows warfare to be a fusion of planning and chance with a generally unpredictable outcome. Brute force and skill interplay, as, in the perception of the participants, do men and Gods.

Many critics have written of the immobility of the novel;[21] but in fact this is at most a feminine characteristic. Salammbô is usually confined to one place, and makes her sortie to retrieve the city's divine robe disguised as a man. The male protagonists, and the armies, are almost constantly on the move, even during periods of siege. The key motif is rather one of restless, pointless or neutralised movement, with one fixed focus, the city, and another itself mobile, since the mercenaries have neither a base on Carthaginian territory nor even a single home to go to (they are drawn from countries all around the Mediterranean).

The war drags on for three years because neither side is able to deliver the *coup de grâce*. In the process, the change of perspective on human nature since *Madame Bovary* – the stress on talent, energy and endeavour – comes to seem less than total, since so many of the positive qualities are deployed to no great effect, as in earlier works. Hamilcar himself fights as if with fingers crossed, hoping for the extra push from fate or the Gods to break the stalemate; though the account of his masterly grip on preparation, tactics, strategy, even psychological warfare, make it clear that Flaubert marks him out as a worthy leader with superior qualities we might associate more readily with characters in Balzac.

A kind of endemic futility is further stressed by repeated episodes of self-destruction: elephants are turned out of control against their own side, and in one elaborate sequence a crack troop of mercenaries are forced to fight each other to the death. The general pattern of the fighting, similarly, is of a series of almost Pyrrhic victories for each side alternately. Furthermore, the whole war is for Carthage an expensive irrelevancy, a parenthesis in its ongoing struggle with Rome for dominance of the central Mediterranean. Flaubert indicates his own cynicism about the dubious relationship between warfare, politics and logic by recording an occasion when Rome itself comes to its old enemy's aid (XIV).

His choice of historical subject-matter proves to have been astute novelistically. The precise conflict is so little known that the reader will always be keen to learn 'what happens next'; and Flaubert deploys a range of narrative devices to keep up the surprise element, concealing motives or tactics, for example. Yet the general context is so well known that only occasional reminders are offered to trigger the reader's awareness that though Carthage will realise much of the 'great hope' evoked at the end, by marching on Rome itself under Hannibal (present here as a Wunderkind), it is his great city, lovingly described in all its conspicuous wealth, which will be totally destroyed.

Flaubert is also at pains to establish a tension between the conventional concept of the military machine as orderly, organised and efficient, and the forces of disorder and anarchy. At first this seems to polarise between the multinational, leaderless 'barbarians', chaotically celebrating and destroying, and the coherence of Carthage. But later we see the mercenaries responding to the central control of their leadership, while the sophisticated collective self-interest of Carthage is menaced by sectional jealousies and power-struggles. This introduces a further theme, that of the interrelation between public and private levels in the characters of the military leaders: the general is also a man. Spendius, enslaved by Carthage, has a personal revenge to take, and therefore lends his Odyssean skills to his mercenary liberators. Mâtho pursues neither wages nor revenge, but a woman who happens to live in Carthage. Hamilcar finally agrees to direct the city's defence less out of patriotism or political self-interest (though both will benefit) than out of personal outrage at the damage done to his estate, his fortune and his family name.

War is also a great collective experience, and Flaubert's portrayal of the masses prefigures the role they will come to play in fiction later in the century. The long series of indecisive battles is reflected in the oscillating moods of the two sides, as well as of their leaders, between confidence and despair. Flaubert sees people in the mass as volatile, easily affected by circumstances, displaying the lowest common denominators of human feeling or thought. Like many intellectuals, he personally disliked, distrusted and feared 'the crowd', and his numerous descriptions in *Salammbô* dwell on its unpleasant, even bestial, features. Though he stresses, on the mercenary side, the diversity of race and custom, he does not share the habit of more democratic, even populist, novelists in isolating ordinary individuals from the mass to give them an identity and a role in the novel's complex of plots. Such features have not endeared the work to Marxist critics, though some ingenuity has been expended recently in presenting the wage-earning mercenaries as Cathage's proletariat, their foreign status symbolising the capitalist exclusion of workers from the ranks of normal humanity, like the many slaves who service the city's peacetime needs.[22]

However, the comparison cannot be taken very far. Although at one point the mercenaries demand Carthaginian brides, their main aim is to return home. The fact that some groups depart, to be replaced in the war by soldiers from states near Carthage, whose motive is very different (they resent the colonisers' power) seems to indicate that Flaubert is more interested in portraying the territorial and colonial wars and economic rivalries of small city states in the third century B.C. than the contradictions of nineteenth-century capitalism. Indeed any convincing analogies with France are more likely to be found in Carthage's status as a commercial and industrial economy in a phase of colonial expansion.

In parallel to his refusal to individualise ordinary soldiers, the picture Flaubert paints of the Carthaginian population is top-heavy, recalling the presentation of state politics in French Classical tragedy. Most attention is lavished on the leaders – Hamilcar, Hannon, Giscon, the priest Schahabarim – and the ruling groups to which they belong. Flaubert's own elitist preferences coincide here with the approach of his Greek and Roman sources to the writing of political history.

Carthage, originally a colony established by Tyre, of the Tigris-Euphrates cradle of Mediterranean civilisation (the Old Testament's Canaan), had become, through mining, industry, trade and colonial aggression, a major force in Mediteranean politics between 700 and 300 B.C. Its expansion brought it into conflict with Greek colonies, then with Rome, notably in the Punic Wars between 264 and 146 B.C. As Flaubert's sources were mainly Greek or Roman, their view of Carthage was of a foreign, alien state and culture. While recognising its wealth, power and highly-organised political, social and religious structures, these sources also presented its people as peculiarly cruel and violent, barbarous. Even in North Africa, the Phoenecians were foreign, incoming colonisers from the East; and Flaubert described alliances between the mercenaries and indigenous peoples. However, in building up his picture from antagonistic sources, Flaubert set himself the technical challenge of taking the reader inside this doubly alien civilisation to show it in its own terms. He eschewed the global modern overview introduction, and kept explanatory interventions to a minimum, scattering them discreetly through the text. Most of the readers' information comes from descriptions of places or people, the actions of protagonists or, more rarely, their words. Thus the historical material is made living and concrete, acquiring that 'reality' Flaubert so conscientiously pursued. The role of the reader is particularly active, since he is obliged to piece together the evidence for himself, as he had to do with *Madame Bovary*.

The initial political situation emerges piecemeal from among the dramatic and spectacular events of the opening chapter; as do the topographical and human structures of the city. The end of Chapter I seems to offer a panoramic overview; but the reader quickly appreciates that there is more to the city than a single look can take in. Other perspectives will be offered, each springing naturally from narrative circumstances and mediated through the angle of vision of a character. The opening presents a mercenary's image of Hamilcar's palace, naïve and envious. When the general

himself returns, we see beneath the luxurious surfaces to the throb-
bing machinery of wealth-creation through agriculture, industry,
commerce, land and property rents and war (VII). The central
position occupied by Hamilcar in our view of the city's economy
is itself significant, for the city is run by an oligarchy made up
of a small number of such rich families, from whom are drawn
the governing assemblies and elected military leaders. The word
Republic, in its limited Classical sense, is a leitmotiv of the text.
Showing its operation through descriptions of assembly meetings,
Flaubert underlines the double fear which haunts the ruling-class:
fear of a threat to its authority from below is relatively insignificant
compared to the fear that an individual from among its own ranks
might seize power, as happened all too often in Classical states.

The civilisation of Carthage emerges as a peculiar mixture of
mysticism and materialism, symbolised by the shape of the city.
As well as its rich palaces, it is dominated by huge temples. Ornate
and ostentatious, they are as much displays of material wealth as
of the power attributed to the divinities. They further double up
as government buildings, showing the interrelation of religion and
politics. The religious element is genuine, and Flaubert stresses
the beliefs of both the crowd and the protagonists. Religion is
polytheistic, though two divinities dominate. Moloch, the male
principle, is associated with the sun, fire and destruction; while
Tanit, the female principle, is associated with the moon, water and
fertility. Their qualities are neatly complementary, Tanit nourishing
the city, while Moloch supports its colonising aggression.

Although in one of his asides Flaubert points out that
Carthaginians confuse the simulacra of the gods with their
intangible essence (III), he refuses to demystify the religion
for the benefit of the unbelieving modern reader. Techniques of
point of view are repeatedly employed to show the Carthaginian
perception; for example of the crucial notion of divine intervention
on the human plane, be it in explanation of Salammbô's illness (III) or
this or that victory or defeat. Tanit's holy robe, lost then recovered,
seems to be accompanied by reversals, then by reinforcements (the
uncertain neighbour Narr-Havas chooses sides) and a significant
victory (XII).

After further reversals, the people turn again to the divine pair
(XIII) and at the end explicitly link the ceremonial slow execution
of Mâtho, the last surviving mercenary, to an act of worship to

the Goddess. Even Hamilcar readily admits the concept of divine interventions, hoping for them in bad times (XIII) and accepting a subordinate role in the final celebrations which enthrone his daughter as a surrogate Goddess and play down his own, human role in assuring victory.

However, despite the initial impression of 'faith', Flaubert's elaborate picture reveals many nuances: fervent belief (Salammbô, Mâtho), puzzled belief (Schahabarim), intermittent and opportunistic belief (Hamilcar and the leaders generally) and downright scepticism (Spendius). Above all, the stress falls on floating, uncertain or intermittent faith. Hamilcar is shown in his first appearance to have a deep religious conviction, whose unconventional, pantheistic form recalls experiences of the young Flaubert; yet he is soon defying the law which bans weapons from the temple-cum-council chamber (VII); later he is accused of pursuing the war in a way which neglects divine law and custom (IX) and will not sacrifice his son to Moloch.

Hamilcar is no Abraham (Flaubert uses numerous Biblical echoes, usually with ironical twists): indeed he exults at feeling 'stronger than the Gods and full of contempt for them' (XIII). The interplay of religious attitudes defies any reductive schema, reflecting the novelist's own uncertain scepticism. On the whole it seems that the barometer of faith rises and falls according to personal need – an unexceptional but no less psychologically reasonable hypothesis. As to the reality of the metaphysical dimension itself, Flaubert follows his own advice, presenting the 'facts', the sequence of events, leaving its interpretation to the participants.

The presentation of Carthage is thus supremely ambiguous in many respects, and especially in the relation between the reader's impression on the one hand of fixity and force, and on the other of weakness and shifting uncertainty. The city's wealth and confidence are menaced by disorder from both without and within. Spendius and Salammbô argue at the outset that its inability to fight its own battles, the origin of the present difficulty, is a sign of its decline; its preference for commercial and industrial rather than military force have made it soft. With its back to the wall it can, just, win a local war; and Flaubert confirms the earlier diagnosis by showing how the ordinary population has to throw its weight behind the final battle (XIV). But the reader knows the fate of Carthage. It is now clear that this extratextual knowledge is a key to the ideas, as well as the narrative strategies, of the novel.

Carthage has been chosen because, despite the superficial image of strength leading to victory, it allows Flaubert to treat one of his favourite historical themes: the moment of crisis when a state, civilisation or religion shows it is not eternal, begins to enter a period of transformation or prepares to disappear. On the religious plane, this had been a major theme of his work on St Antony, and it is noticeable in the novel that the firm believers die, while others move to a more sceptical attitude, and Spendius dies convinced that there is nothing beyond earthly life itself (XIV). The priest Schahabarim, seeking, like St Antony, the answers to fundamental metaphysical questions, only grows more confused; he changes his allegiance to the male divinity just in time for the fickle population to switch its favour to Tanit.

The general theme of decadence is manifest also in the prominence of such factors as gratuitous, institutionalised cruelty, repeatedly shown to be materially counterproductive: Hamilcar, in a rage, punishes his slaves, though he has just demonstrated the economic nonsense this makes (VII); captured enemy troops are slaughtered when they might have been encouraged to change sides or have been bartered for Carthaginian prisoners (IX). The rising curve of insensibility, culminates in a final scene where the people, having at last fought its own battle, takes on, less nobly, the role of torturer in putting Mâtho to death with its own hands. In the complex interplay of parallel and contrast between the opening and closing scenes, the 'civilised' population act as irrationally, emotionally and destructively at the end as the 'barbarians' did at the beginning, with the same motive, blind revenge. It is clear too that this negative Carthaginian human image is projected and magnified in their divinities. The anthropomorphism of religions generally was one of Flaubert's main objections to them. Carthage's Gods are cruel, ambiguous powers, notably fickle, hungry for material gratifications such as luxury and for physical signs of respect and submission. They dominate the whole city as the rich dominate the rest of the population or the powerful leaders dominate the ruling class. Symbols of forces of nature which are beyond human control (sun, moon, the elements), they also incarnate natural forces within man, notably sexuality and aggression.

*

Turning finally to the third major element of the novel – the love story – we find obvious links with the other two. Sexuality and aggression will play key roles, as also will such dichotomies as fixity/change, assurance/decadence, or balance/disequilibrium. The links will be stressed in the text: for example, the analogies with the nature of the divinities are integrated by having the two lovers frequently perceived as closely related to the Gods, even earthly images or extensions of them.

The eponymous heroine is the most totally-imagined of the characters; Polybius notes only that Hamilcar rewarded an ally by offering his daughter in marriage. The hero-lover, Mâtho, figures more prominently in history as the mercenary leader who is last to be killed (no doubt the detail that caught Flaubert's attention). Flaubert gives him two personal attributes: his passionate fixation on Salammbô, and a sincere, if loosely-focused, religious faith. These blend neatly, so that he comes to identify the beloved with the Goddess she serves. Salammbô in turn tends to identify him with the military and destructive God Moloch. This highlights the superior status and stature of this novel's lovers compared to Flaubert's nineteenth-century protagonists. The characteristic 'apparition' which initiates the romantic obsession of a Charles Bovary or a Frédéric Moreau with an attractive but relatively ordinary female takes on a heroic, indeed hieratic, form.

Salammbô's first appearance has the trappings of a grand spectacle; and she exercises a hypnotic effect on all the mercenaries. Her songs and lamentations, as well as her apparent gifts as a linguist (she chats to the soldiers in their own tongues), further set her apart from Flaubert's other heroines, who are poor communicators. But chance and misunderstanding play their usual role. In pouring a drink for Mâtho she intends it as a gesture of peace and conciliation. It is wrongly interpreted by a foreign bystander, a Gaul, as a promise of sexual submission, thus precipitating a conflict of jealous rivalry with Narr-Havas, a non-mercenary guest of Hamilcar.

Salammbô flees the violence, and Mâtho's pursuit is thwarted by the physical barriers of the palace, as it will be repeatedly thwarted by the walls and gates of the city for the rest of the novel. Mâtho will be unmoved by Spendius' military and economic way of looking at the same features. Distracted, 'immensely troubled' by this brief vision, he makes this passion, duly attributed to an act of the Gods, the unique driving force of his life. It takes on a doubly contradictory form. His desire to possess her is alternately violent and tender; but he is also at times overcome with a desire to submit to *her* will, to accept his enslavement. The alternations echo the oscillating moods of crowds and individuals in the military conflict, and resemble the way all the human figures alternately submit to the power of the divinities or seek to manipulate or direct them. But they also relate Mâtho to Flaubert's modern psychology in Emma, or later Frédéric Moreau. And like them he will be a prey to reverie or intense memory-experiences.

The main facets of Mâtho's love are exemplified in the daring two-man raid on the city to steal Tanit's sacred robe and weaken the divine protection. Mâtho's secret hope is to use it to control the Goddess' servant, and having stolen it he proceeds to her quarters, claiming that she has mysteriously summoned him, but advancing to possess her in his own right, crying 'I love you'. But the cup-episode has set the pattern of their relations: mutual misunderstanding based on a fundamental difference between their interests and motives, at least on the conscious level. Salammbô, to whose feelings for Mâtho the word 'love' will never once be attributed throughout the novel, is obsessed with the robe, which she has longed to see and touch as a way of satisfying her thirst to know more about the Goddess whom she serves. Brought up almost as a vestal virgin, she is hence associated with just one aspect of the polyvalent Goddess, who variously represents virginity, sexuality and fertility. She is now suffering from a mysterious illness, the sexual roots of which emerge for the modern reader through Flaubert's studiously Carthaginian diagnosis:

> But the jealous Goddess was taking her vengeance on this virginity which had been kept away from her sacrifices, and she tormented Salammbô with obsessions all the more strong by reason of their vagueness, obsessions which permeated the girl's belief and were stirred up by it. (III)

But however prescient in his dramatisation of repression, Flaubert is not Freud, and he refuses to reduce the metaphysical to the sexual. When, in her confrontation with Mâtho (V), she trembles with horror on sensing that he wants something other than the robe, but outside her comprehension, the reader may see a certain compatibility between her vague desires and his. But it is also quite comprehensible that, confronted by a military and religious enemy of her people, she should utter a solemn triple curse against him. Three hundred pages later Mâtho will be torn, smothered and burned, as she had willed, subtly confirming, for the alert reader, the congratulations of the priests who call his death 'her handiwork' (XV). Meanwhile, Mâtho escapes with the robe.

A further misunderstanding arises when Hamilcar confronts his daughter. Told that she 'takes lovers among the Mercenaries', and tied by an unwise (but narratorially convenient) oath, he is unable to get at the truth in a scene perilously close to the comic or melodramatic *quid pro quo* of nineteenth-century theatre. He interprets as guilt for a sexual crime that which she feels for 'the sacrilege in which she was implicated', that is the theft of the robe (VII). This misunderstanding constitutes a contributory factor in Hamilcar's decision to resume command and defeat the mercenaries. The interrelation of the main strands of the novel is further stressed when Salammbô is persuaded to undertake a mission to retrieve the robe by Schahabarim, who has his personal, religious reasons for wanting it back. He and the reader are aware that if necessary Salammbô's sexuality will be used. She has no grasp of this, and she carries out a preparatory ritual dance involving a holy python with only the vaguest instinctive sense of its erotic symbolism (X).

The second confrontation with Mâtho, this time in his tent, is a neat structural inversion of the first. Salammbô advances to claim the robe, forcing herself to allow him to hold and gaze at her, revealing the fascination she feels for him in an elegant flood of words which he poetically matches. Despite this display of superiority over the tongue-tied or cliché-babbling lovers of *Madame Bovary*, the couple's viewpoints and goals remain as incompatible as any in the earlier novel. However, although Salammbô, caught up in the physiological and psychological effects of Mâtho's erotic presence, feels herself softening and swooning, like Emma before her (*M.B.* II, x), she never loses sight of her religious and patriotic purpose. Mâtho, after oscillating between his desires to dominate and to submit, and breaking the ornamental chain which symbolises her virginity, eventually drifts off into a contented sleep. Salammbô's actions are somewhat incoherent. She quickly dismisses her embarrassment at finding her chastity chain broken, but her impulse to kill him is thwarted by circumstance and forgotten in its turn as he is called away to a skirmish. Alone, she achieves her obsessive goal of knowledge by touching and studying the robe. It has nothing to offer, and she feels 'melancholy at having attained her dream' (XI). There remains the military value, though, and she carries the robe triumphantly to her father's beleaguered camp. He can hardly misunderstand her motives this time, though as father he must come to terms with the broken chain, disposing of the damaged goods to his unsuspecting new ally, Narr-Havas.

Despite the betrayal, Mâtho remains obsessed with Salammbô, and the war continues to be a personal matter. Her development is potentially more interesting. Her sickness gone, she is calm and less worried by religious questions. No explanation is offered, though the reader may conclude that a double tension – erotic and metaphysical – has been resolved. Hatred seems to have mellowed into an ambiguous curiosity as she gazes at the mercenary camp; her attitude to the events in the tent, indeed her memory of them, is fogged (XIII). Unfortunately she then disappears from the text for long periods and her development is neglected. Brief scenes evoke her attitude to Narr-Havas, whose youthful and somewhat feminine figure hardly squares with 'maleness' as her experience of Mâtho has revealed it. Yet she now wills the death of the mercenary: it seems to her the only way of ridding her consciousness of his obsessive presence (XIV).

Mâtho is taken alive – by Narr-Havas – so she must confront him once more. Magnetised by the sight, she superimposes on his torn body the memory of his tenderness in the tent: 'she did not want him to die!' Too late. Even now, consistent with her formation and her level of understanding, she does not think in terms of love. Indeed she seems not to think at all, and is led, 'almost unconscious', back to her throne to watch the ceremonial removal of Mâtho's heart and the joy of the city; Narr-Havas makes a formal gesture of possession and drinks 'to the genius of Carthage'. Before Salammbô can reciprocate she falls backwards off the throne. Struck down by what force? The text will only say:

> Thus died the daughter of Hamilcar because she had touched the robe of Tanit.

A disarming simplicity, compared to the multitude of pressures driving Emma to take her own life. But Flaubert had insisted that the two women were totally unalike precisely in that Emma's passion was many-sided while Salammbô's was obsessively single (V, 58). The absence of any material cause of death is striking in a novel where thousands of deaths had been as clinically described and explained as Emma's. For all the ingenuity of modern critics – one feminist claims that in some way Salammbô commits suicide to thwart her father's use of her as a political chattel[23] – the text admits only the idea of divine punishment. She had after all been warned, long before uttering her own curse on Mâtho which has just been fulfilled. When in only her second appearance in the novel, she asks the priest 'will I see the Goddess?', he replies:

> Never. Do you not know that to do so means death? . . . Your desire is a sacrilege; be content with the knowledge you possess! (III)

Even a cursory statistical breakdown of the distribution of themes across the 400 pages of *Salammbô* would justify the disappointment of those early reviewers who, defining 'novel' as the study of the human heart, regretted that the author of *Madame Bovary* had turned to a subject dominated by war and topography. Salammbô figures in less than one-fifth of the text, reversing the ratio in *Madame Bovary*; and even those pages are often devoted to externals, especially to costumes described so fully that they inspired a Paris fashion. Moreover, she is present on barely twenty of the last 150 pages, and Flaubert himself acknowledged that 'the pedestal is bigger than the statue', which would have needed another hundred pages to do it justice (V, 69). Analysis of all the protagonists, and inner monologue, are at a premium; point of view technique is used to integrate descriptions of places and events more than to illuminate character; dialogue occupies a mere ten per cent of the text – a record low for Flaubert – and is often devoted to political debate or military strategy.

Overall, the approach to characterisation looks forward to the late tales in the relative imbalance between extensive descriptions of appearance and gesture and almost laconic presentation of word, thought or feeling. Flaubert remains true to his general principle that each work imposes its own form and techniques. The protagonists of *Salammbô* share with those of *Trois Contes* an almost monomaniacal simplicity. They too illustrate the central paradox of an intensely physical life coexisting with a deep spirituality within or immediately around it. Their psychological make up seems to fall either well short of, or well beyond, the analytical capacities of language itself. We have seen that Flaubert manages to show characters evolving in time under the pressure of experience, and to indicate their oscillation between contradictory impulses or feelings. But this remains an outline, compared to the nuanced details of Emma's inner life; and perhaps a method better adapted to short fiction than to the long novel.

The final impression is thus very mixed, and may explain the relative neglect of this work by the general reader and, until very recently, the critic. There is much to admire in the successful handling of a complex of major themes, their clever interrelation at various levels, the resolution of a number of technical challenges, the organisation of a narrative which will at once surprise the reader by its twists and turns and yet communicate a sense of inevitability. A dead civilisation is so convincingly recreated that for many years commentators accepted the novel's total detachment from any contemporary relevance outside the disturbing contours of Flaubert's own psyche. In recent years, as we saw, critics have shown signs of reacting too far in the opposite direction, reading the novel as a coded commentary on Second Empire France. Certainly Flaubert projects a general image which would fit both historical moments: a society full of confidence in itself heading nevertheless for decline and death. But the continuing applicability of some themes into the late twentieth century – especially the absurdities of war – suggest that Flaubert's real conclusion was the eminently Classical perception of permanent features in the structures of society as of Man.

Yet the reader cannot but feel that Flaubert's divided interest – perhaps exacerbated by a lack of confidence in his grasp of the psychology of pre-Christian man – has shifted the centre of gravity of the work. In his extensive exploration of a society and a war Flaubert seems to be taking the novel form towards the type of panoramic social study which would shortly be undertaken by the young Emile Zola and the so-called Naturalist novelists. They, too, in portraying individuals caught up in great social movements, tend to favour external, physical, even physiological methods rather than the traditional inner analysis. Zola too will portray a confident, but doomed, materialistic society; he too will be drawn to the extremes of human experience in the individual as in the crowd. Although

the nineteenth-century passion for encyclopaedias and the vulgari-
sation of knowledge found its echo in all the successive 'realistic'
schools or theories of fiction in France, each had its own methods.
Zola followed Flaubert in the discreet and dramatic integration of
'factual', documentary material into a strong narrative framework.
His subject was, of course, the Second Empire itself, not a dead
civilisation. When Flaubert returned to a modern setting, however,
even though his thematic aim was ambitious and his chosen period
dramatic, involving Revolution, mass revolt and the collapse of two
régimes, he reverted to many of the features of *Madame Bovary*, as we
shall see in the next chapter.

6

L'Education Sentimentale

After completing *Salammbô*, Flaubert undertook another ambiguous flight from reality, composing rapidly with friends a *féerie* (a kind of adult pantomime) called *Le Château des Coeurs*. The ambiguity lay in the play's serious human theme: the loss of the heart, the capacity to feel, in the modern world. But the important business was to find a theme for a realistic novel of modern life. In the autumn of 1864 he wrote that it would be the 'moral', or more accurately 'sentimental' (i.e. affective) story of 'the men of my generation', and he set it in Paris in the 1840s (V, 158).

A substantial historical and political element would carry on the trend set by *Salammbô*, but in other ways the project represented the inevitable reaction. The dominant theme would be not politics but love and, what is more, 'passion as it can exist now, that is to say inactive' (V, 158). During the five year composition period there were the usual complaints about the boring or irritating aspects of the work, coupled with the usual relentless thoroughness in documentation, planning and writing. The manuscript dossiers show with striking clarity his renewed aim to hide the psychology (and much else) 'under the form': elaborate psychological or political analyses disappear between the plans and the final text, leaving only the 'picture'.[24]

Flaubert came to regret, as he worked, his decision to embed a fictional love story involving ordinary people (another contrast with *Salammbô*) in real events. He was sure the reader would be more interested in the historical figures, who this time were only part of the background (V, 363). Furthermore, the protagonists were too 'soft' (*mou*), insufficiently passionate and too complicated to grab the attention. 'But', he complained, 'I see simplicity nowhere in the modern world' (V, 331). He exchanged ideas with the radical feminist writer George Sand about the period leading up to the

1848 Revolution, the brief Second Republic and Louis-Napoleon's *coup d'état* of December 1851 which ushered in the Second Empire. Though like her he had no sympathy for the Right, he had a low opinion of Republican and Socialist thought. As well as rejecting its levelling principle of equality (which he called 'slavery') he resented what he saw as its religious roots and Messianic tone, absurdly unfitted to a scientific age. But he had no intention of stating these opinions openly in the novel. He sought, he said, 'to express what seems to me the truth', and went on:

> Rich or poor, winners or losers, I admit none of that. I want to have neither love nor hate, pity nor anger. As for sympathy, that's a different matter – you can never have enough of that. (VI, 68, 1868)

Completed in May 1869, the novel sold well when it appeared in November, but the critical reception was hostile. It was considered politically radical, and also found lacking in structure and plan. Flaubert gained a wry consolation from the fact that readers claimed to recognise real-life models for his heavily-satirised secondary characters, naming people he had never even met, and thus confirming the 'truth' of his painstakingly reconstituted 'picture'.

The 'Paris novel', as Flaubert had called it in his correspondence, was almost complete when, in April 1869, he wrote to George Sand:

> Talking of titles, you promised to find one for my novel, here is what I have chosen, in desperation:
> Sentimental Education
> Story of a young man (Sup. II, 175)

He had mentioned the title *L'Education Sentimentale* while preparing the first plans (Sup. I, 321). He also considered *Les Fruits Secs* (Dry fruit), but finally opted, as with his other works, for the matter-of-fact phrases, which would acquire resonances only after the text had been read. Though situating his work in that substantial nineteenth-century category 'the novel of education', the title and subtitle seem to neglect the social, political and intellectual facets of learning which were so important to earlier French practitioners such as Stendhal or Balzac. The basic starting-point, however, respects the established tradition: the provincial student arrives in Paris,

ambitious to succeed on all fronts. Though a cliché of fiction by the
1860s, it was firmly rooted in fact, due to the extreme centralisation
of political and financial power, society and artistic life, and even
higher education itself. Balzac's earlier use of the theme is openly
exploited by Flaubert, but for ironic effect: his young men's attempt
to model themselves on Balzac's heroes is both unconvincing and
unsuccessful.

Frédéric Moreau has just qualified for university in a provincial
school and is advised by his best friend Deslauriers to imitate
Balzac's Rastignac (the hero of *Le Père Goriot*) by exploiting his con-
tacts and his charm as well as his intelligence to get on socially and
financially. In contrast to Deslauriers, the embittered and ambitious
son of a failed minor legal official, Frédéric has had a reasonable
start in life. His school career showed promise, he hopes for a large
inheritance from a rich uncle, and his widowed mother, though
living in genteel poverty, is of aristocratic origins which attract
respect in their home town of Nogent, sixty-five miles south east
of Paris. But Frédéric's personality has none of the single-minded
will and determination of Balzac's successful young provincials. He
is dreamy, passive, fatalistic. Imbued with the Romantic literature of
disenchantment (we are in 1840) he proclaims himself 'of the race of
the disinherited' (I,ii) and at eighteen expects to fail both in love and
in his vocation. These temperamental limitations are compounded
when, on the river steamer between Paris and Montereau, an attractive young mother, Madame Arnoux, appears 'like an apparition' (I,i).
It is love at first sight, as with Charles Bovary or Mâtho. But these
older men had already had some 'sentimental education' whereas
Frédéric, like Emma, though steeped in the literature of love, is completely inexperienced. The initial physical impact quickly spreads to
his emotions and imagination with a very real intensity which, as
throughout the novel, is conveyed by the use of a simple hyperbole:

> (. . .) even the desire for physical possession disappeared beneath
> a deeper longing, in a painful curiosity that was boundless. (I, i)

A key metaphor quickly follows, expressing a theme central to
all the novel's relationships:

> The more he gazed at her, thhe more he felt abysses open
> up between them.

It is difficult, in the light of these recurring motifs, as of many other features of the description of Frédéric's inner life, to share the opinion of those critics who insist that Frédéric never really loved anyone.[25] The hyperboles and the 'abysses' stand out all the more in the text as Flaubert, who had declared his intention of having 'no metaphors' (Sup. II, 100), did, in fact, employ much less and much simpler figurative language than in *Madame Bovary*, draining his style of colour and vitality to make it echo the work's central themes. Frédéric's response to the 'apparition' is both a key to the themes of this novel and an example of the continuity of Flaubert's psychology since *Madame Bovary*. For he evokes a compensatory dream of togetherness so vivid that it all but merges into the reality before his eyes; indeed in later episodes the narrator will use the word 'hallucination'. At the end of the journey the memory Frédéric calls up is as vivid and precise, creating a strange yet satisfying sense of dilation, at once of the world around him and of his own self. All this comes from the mere contemplation of a woman with whom he has exchanged few words and about whom he has learnt far less than about her gregarious and loose-tongued husband, a Paris art-dealer and publisher.[26]

But contemplation is perhaps the key to love in Frédéric's passive temperament, and memory and dream more important than real contact. Though Frédéric shortly moves to Paris to study law, he shows none of the boldness of Rastignac, and it is only during his second year that chance, which proves the chief organiser of his life throughout the novel,[27] begins to smile on him. A witty young journalist, Hussonnet, reintroduces him to Arnoux, and a second meeting with his wife renews Frédéric's experience of dilation and exaltation: he even hopes she will inspire him to great things. But soon he faces the rivalry of love and friendship, for Deslauriers joins him in Paris, thus setting up the first of a series of triangles involving Frédéric, Madame Arnoux and '*l'autre*' (the other man or woman).

Frédéric learns that abysses can also separate close friends, for Deslauriers, whose idea of love is pragmatic and physical, fails to grasp the nature of his comrade's Romantic obsession (echoes, here, of the relations between Mâtho and Spendius). Nonetheless Deslauriers offers advice, tries to distract Frédéric with male companionship and even tries to find a suitable partner. Inhibited by his fixation, Frédéric is briefly tempted by suicide (I, v). Chance intervenes again to bring him back into Arnoux's circle where he begins to form some impression of Madame Arnoux's personality. Firm and upright, but sensitive, she is no Romantic superior soul, and her conventional morality invites the scorn of modern critics. But she does not act basely, selfishly or inconsistently and can be seen as a reverse, positive, image of 'Madame' Bovary in her role as a wife and mother. A casual word from her stimulates again Frédéric's feeling of dilation and drives him on to success in his exams. Social progress is promised when Frédéric falls in with a rich politician, Monsieur Dambreuse, whose agent in Nogent, Roche, is his mother's neighbour.

The wheel of fortune then turns sharply as Madame Moreau's deteriorating financial situation obliges her to interrupt Frédéric's studies. He briefly threatens to imitate the Balzacian model, but home comforts prove more attractive than a Paris garret, and he sinks into a disappointing idleness, diverting himself with the education of the twelve-year-old Louise Roche, whose spontaneity and authenticity of feeling have escaped the distortions of convent education. He is rewarded by an adoring worship that shows signs of precocious erotic fixation. Meanwhile his own great love, like Emma's for Rodolphe after his betrayal, is entombed in his memory, apparently forgotten, but susceptible to the right trigger.

Years pass before the rich uncle dies, leaving Frédéric a substantial fortune. The news immediately throws him into a daydream whose imprecision reflects his uncertainty as to the kind of relationship he may now establish with Madame Arnoux (I, vi). The intensity of the feeling is, however, confirmed by a feverish return to Paris and a desperate quest for her, Arnoux's dubious speculations having forced them to move to more modest quarters. While she has grown more domesticated, with a second child, Arnoux has acquired as mistress a successful and popular courtesan, Rosanette, destined to be '*l'autre*' in one of Frédéric's triangles. Indeed he becomes the confidant of two contrasting, but equally inhibiting women. Madame Arnoux's stern morality generates a respect which the narrator, in a rare evaluative judgement, calls 'prodigious cowaarrdice' (II, ii), while Rosanetttte's camaraderie completely desexualises his relations with her. Chance keeps him hopping between them and Deslauriers, though when crises loom Frédéric's hesitations are resolved in the Arnoux's favour; they get 15,000 francs promised for one of Deslaurier's schemes (II, iii). After Madame Arnoux has come in person to deliver another plea for help, Frédéric lags well behind the reader in suspecting that his susceptibility is being exploited by her husband. His general failure to see clearly, interpret and explain what is happening around him, is a further inversion of the Balzac type, who is richly endowed with *his* creator's perspicacity.

Another weakness is revealed in a Romantic confrontation with Madame Arnoux. Though he now both loves and desires her intensely, his 'inactivity' and his 'softness' make him wrap up his declaration in literary generalities, and he is easily crushed by her cool refusal to admit love outside marriage. The twin devices of vague hyperbole and metaphor of depths recur:

> He felt at first an infinite stupefaction. This way of making him see the pointlessness of his hope crushed him. He felt lost like a man who has fallen into an abyss, who knows that no help will come and that he must die. (II, iii)

He has no more luck in his sensual pursuit of Rosanette, who in an admirable set-piece description of the races chooses his stupid, but richer, and aristocratic friend de Cisy. Yet it is about Madame Arnoux that the two men fight an absurd duel shortly after, despite the fact that what Proust might have called 'the intermittences' of Frédéric's heart have again turned him away from his idol. A stock market success encourages his society ambitions, but the Balzacian model is parodied: after a blunder on his first visit to Dambreuse's salon, he drifts back into Deslauriers' bachelor circle, and when he loses all his profits retreats to Nogent. There the frank approaches of Louise, now a nubile teenager, leave him as nonplussed as the indifference of the two Parisiennes, and he flees back to the city, only to find Rosanette transformed and just as embarrassingly encouraging. But an accidental, insignificant, street meeting with Madame Arnoux underlines the difference in both nature and intensity of his attachment to her:

> She hadn't preferred her hand, hadn't said a single affectionate word, hadn't even invited him to call. No matter! He would not have exchanged that meeting for the most beautiful adventure, and he ruminated on how sweet it had been as he continued on his way. (II, vi)

At their next meeting, her comments about the other women in his life drive him to a spontaneous protestation of love:

> And, taking her hand in both his hands, he began to kiss her on the eyes, repeating:
> 'No! No! No! I will never marry! never! never!'
> She accepted these caresses, frozen by surprise and delight. (ib)

Next day the force of Frédéric's renewed avowals (clichés, but sincerely meant, like so many of Emma's) weakens her resolve, but she begs him to leave:

> And Frédéric loved her so much that he left. (ib)

Her subsequent flight to a country cottage is a clear avowal of the struggle between her love and her austere conventional morality, and a passionately platonic friendship develops, feeding on memories and dreams. But repressed physical desire builds up in Frédéric once winter brings her back to Paris, and he eventually plans a seduction in a specially rented apartment. It is February 1848 and revolt breaks out in the streets; but it is her son's illness, perceived as a moral warning, which prevents her keeping the rendezvous. In his fury he finds an unexpected force and will-power to overcome the mitigated resistance of Rosanette and his own virginity. This seems for a time to have exorcised the spell cast by Madame Arnoux nearly eight years before, and he enjoys the company of Rosanette so much that he is playing the tourist honeymooner with her at Fontainebleau when violence again sweeps Paris in June.

The idyll has negative undercurrents. Frédéric is irritated by Rosanette's lack of culture and her rapid disenchantment with a Republic whose anarchic incompetence, by sapping wealth and economic confidence, threatens her profession as much as any legitimate business. Even the happier moments are undermined by deceit and non-communication, pointed by one of the narrator's few generalising interventions, notably gloomier than the similar comment made in *Madame Bovary*:

> . . . in the middle of the most intimate sharing of secrets there are always restrictions, caused by false shame, delicacy or pity. We discover in the other person (l'autre) or in ourselves precipices

or miry expanses which prevent us from going on; besides, we feel we would not be understood; it is difficult to express precisely anything at all; therefore complete unions are rare. (III, i)

Frédéric's life remains profoundly divided. In June he is torn between love and friendship, when he briefly abandons Rosanette to return to the embattled capital to help his wounded Republican friend Dussardier. Later he is torn by conflicting loves. In 1846 Flaubert had argued to Louise Colet that men were not only capable of loving in different ways, but of doing so at the same time (Plé I, 328). Frédéric, while enjoying his erotic possession of Rosanette, has his ego flattered by the adoring attention of Louise, who boldly comes to Paris to seek him out; and he even flirts with Madame Dambreuse. Yet despite Madame Arnoux's refusal of him in February 1848, he has not forgotten her, nor lost hope, nor ceased to dream (III, i).

When they meet, in company, she is cold and he turns against her (III, ii). This 'intermittence' does not last, and in February 1849 they are together again, the relationship progressing quickly. But though this time she responds – 'they embraced tightly, standing there, in a long kiss' (III, iii) – he meekly allows Rosanette to lead him away, and thereafter seeks to substitute another kind of love, rooted in vanity and tinged with both eroticism and social ambition, for Madame Dambreuse. This relationship, too, exposes Frédéric's 'softness', for she yields to him only when it suits her. By the time her husband dies, early in 1851, and she proposes that they legitimise their liaison, the sensual attraction has faded, but her wealth and social position make her a good match. When he accepts, though, it is out of fatuously self-regarding 'nobility' (echoing Emma's role-playing), for he has learnt that she has inherited little of her husband's fortune. His failure to act ruthlessly in his own interest – financial or sentimental – is highlighted by the parallel manoeuvres of Deslauriers, who after trying to seduce Madame Arnoux, then to ingratiate himself with Dambreuse, sets his sights on Louise, in all cases, of course, exploiting his privileged position as Frédéric's friend.

Frédéric by now resembles a protagonist in a classic farce, embodying rather more of the 'grotesque' than of the 'pathos' in Flaubert's ambiguous view of the human condition. Father of Rosanette's child – and she too is angling for marriage –

he divides his day between her and Madame Dambreuse, while being drawn into a network of money problems rich in ironic reversals and theatrical misunderstandings. Rosanette, for example, has scarcely been helped to escape a creditor herself when she joins those pursuing Arnoux. Learning that Arnoux has little chance of staving off prosecution and is likely to flee Paris, Frédéric gets his affections into perspective:

> He needed 12,000 francs or he would never see Madame Arnoux again; and up to now he had kept an invincible hope. Was she not, so to speak, the very substance of his heart, the very basis of his life? For several minutes he stood tottering on the pavement, consumed with anguish, yet happy that he was no longer with the other woman [Rosanette]. (III, v)

Drama merges into black comedy as he is obliged to borrow the money from Madame Dambreuse, to whom chance reveals the intended beneficiary. Though he has been too late to stop the Arnoux's flight, and returned her money, she secretly plans her revenge, by having their property seized to settle some unpaid debts. Accusing Rosanette of this outrage Frédéric, in the heat of the quarrel, at last articulates a kind of self-awareness on the affective plane, declaring:

> 'I have never loved anyone but her.' (III, v)

Since in the nineteenth century marriage was perceived as having little to do with love, the plans for his wedding with Madame Dambreuse proceed, precipitating what the narrator calls a 'revolution' in Nogent: we are in late November 1851. On December 1st, Madame Arnoux's effects are sold off. Miscalculating badly, Madame Dambreuse insists on buying a box which is linked to some of Frédéric's fondest memories. It is his turn to revolt, avenging Madame Arnoux by leaving Madame Dambreuse; only to find that his life, after being filled with women for so long, is now empty and aimless. On December 2nd, Napoleon's *coup d'état* puts an end to the Second Republic, though Frédéric's interest in the matter is even lower than in the Revolutions of 1848. The real blow for him is the discovery, two days later, that Louise has married Deslauriers, leaving him completely alone.

Whereas Emma was in a way killed by Rodolphe's second rejection of her, Frédéric's 'sentimental' life is permanently crippled by the absence of any such final resolution of his love for Madame Arnoux. His middle age is so hollow that Flaubert can summarise it in twelve lines (III, vi). He is forty-five, she well past fifty, when she unexpectedly visits him again, to repay an old loan. Memory stirs up the old magic, but the present is more ambiguous. Though her white hair is a disappointing shock, the closeness and apparent availability of her body draw him towards a gesture so often avoided or thwarted in the past:

> However he felt something inexpressible, a repulsion, and something resembling the terror of committing an incest. Another fear stopped him, that of being disgusted by it afterwards. Besides, how embarrassing it would be! And both out of prudence and in order not to degrade his ideal he turned on his heels and began to roll a cigarette. (III, vi)

She leaves, saying they will never meet again, though making clear that her love will not fade.

As during their younger days, Frédéric and Deslauriers eventually find each other, 'reconciled', says the narrator, 'yet again by the fatality of their nature which made them constantly draw back together in friendship.' (III, vii). Most of their acquaintances have failed or changed for the worse, illustrating the author's pessimistic vision of universal mediocrity. Even Frédéric's Romantic fixation on Madame Arnoux seems finally to have faded away. The excuses he and Deslauriers advance for their general lack of success in life, though unconsciously ironic, are more ambiguous than is sometimes recognised. Frédéric's life has indeed 'lacked a straight line', drifting aimlessly among four women, male camaraderie and a variety of artistic and political ambitions. Yet it has been dominated by a single factor, Madame Arnoux, from their first meeting to their last.

Deslauriers had, as he claims, more energy and directness than his friend; but his line of conduct shows all the curves of opportunism. There is less authorial irony behind their joint accusation of 'chance, circumstances, the period in which they were born'. For without the cushion of unearned income Frédéric would not have had the leisure to dream, to be always available for the next twist of fate; while with more solid social and financial support

Deslauriers' energy might have built a success, like that of their fellow-student Martinon, who adds to the Dambreuse fortune, acquired by marriage, a political career in the Senate. The novel does not end with these general considerations, for the friends slide into precise memories of their school days, culminating in a secret visit to Nogent's notorious brothel, a visit which came to nothing because a complex combination of circumstances made Frédéric, faced by a roomful of girls, flee in embarrassment. The reference, beyond the events described in the opening chapter, to the period covered by a short flashback in I, ii, is clearly intended to give the narrative structure a clinching element of circularity to set against the more obvious linear movement through some thirty years of Frédéric's life. Much ingenuity has been expended by critics seeking other layers of significance for a scene which the protagonists themselves, looking back, consider 'the best thing that ever happened' to them. It is tempting to see the remark as putting all the experiences recounted in the novel in a kind of parenthesis, just as the Punic Wars reduce the action of *Salammbô* to a parenthesis. It is often argued that the title-word 'education' is massively ironic because the friends have learned nothing; though it might be more correct to say that they have been unable to profit from the lessons they have learned through an inability to *act* effectively, for a variety of reasons internal and external.

Their final judgement, though as ambiguous as anything else in this novel, does have its value. 'Best' perhaps relates to the fact that because they did not achieve their desired goal they escaped on that privileged occasion the disappointments of Emma, Salammbô or, later, Bouvard and Pécuchet when they achieved theirs. But 'perhaps' remains the operrative word, for the text neatly sidesteps any explicit confirmation. Indeed, after *Madame Bovary*, whose finale is clear enough, leaving Charles dead of a broken heart and the heartless Monsieur Homais in command in Yonville, all Flaubert's endings, while marked by structural circularity, will have a teasing openness about them, not through any lack of narrative finality (the main characters die or reach the end of their active lives) but through the avoidance of any explanations. Flaubert plays off his passion for perfection – which etymologically implies completeness – against his rejection of 'conclusions' in a thoroughly modern manner.

Despite the titles, the novel is of course not just a 'book of love', the story of Frédéric's feelings. His role is double, in that he serves not only as psychological subject, like Emma, but also as eyewitness, like Antoine. Some of the principal features of his biography are narrative expedients, giving verisimilitude to the latter function. Deslauriers gradually introduces him to the Republican and Socialist opposition to the July Monarchy, while family connections and his legacy assure his acceptance among businessmen who support the régime. Even his Romantic fixation is exploited, since Arnoux draws him into the worlds of the arts and of courtesans. The minor characters are primarily mouthpieces for typical social, political or aesthetic attitudes, expressed mainly through conversations with, or in the presence of, Frédéric, whose viewpoint, in the physical sense, is used for over seventy per cent of the text.[28]

This 'point of view' approach allows Flaubert systematically to interrelate and fuse both the diverse character groups and milieux, and the themes they represent, a feature reinforced by the narrative pattern itself, which constantly alternates or combines Frédéric's roles as protagonist and pretext. In Part I Chapter iv he first watches with almost complete detachment a street riot, then frequents Arnoux's office, where the psychological dimension of his secret interest in the publisher's wife shares the attention with a gallery of representative figures from the art world; when he finally visits Arnoux's home his state of mind dominates as he gazes on the 'apparition', but his mere presence allows Flaubert to record a lively aesthetic debate between the other guests. The reader thus acquires a vivid sense of Frédéric being embedded in a complex 'reality', being a part of his time, however personally uninterested he is in it, however independent the main current of his life may be of real historical events.

Yet because there is only one viewpoint, and because it is that of an ordinary citizen, the reader's grasp of the period itself is much more limited than in *Salammbô*. Flaubert makes few attempts to complement Frédéric's knowledge with that of an omniscient narrator, in striking contrast to Tolstoy's double approach in *War and Peace*, written at much the same time. The precise historical allusions, realistically dropped in conversations, are rarely elucidated, and must sometimes have puzzled Flaubert's contemporaries, so detailed and recondite were his researches. But then, as professional historians of the period have noted, Flaubert's aim is to provide neither a chronological history nor a serious political, economic and social analysis, but a psychological and ideological picture of the time.[29] It is clear from his correspondence that it was to psychology and ideology that Flaubert turned for his own explanation of both the general spirit and the precise evolution of the 1840s.

It might be expected, then, that Frédéric would have a third important function as a representative in himself of some aspect of the ideological conflicts. In fact, this aspect of his education is somewhat muffled, in contrast to the clear outline of the hardening political stance of Deslauriers during the period. Despite the loquacity of spokesmen of Left and Right to whom he listens, Frédéric ventures few words, and has even fewer reported thoughts, on politics till 1848. Although his background is Conservative, he seems more in sympathy with the ideals of the Left, and on one occasion loses patience with the self-seeking 'rottenness' of Dambreuse and his cronies (II, iv). Frédéric's duel for Madame Arnoux's honour takes place in the same chapter, and it is easy to see, here and elsewhere in the text, that the juxtaposition is intended to highlight the close thematic links between Frédéric's Romantic fixation and a symmetrically vague, impractical idealism in politics.

In 1848 politics, by descending into the street and violently overthrowing a régime, thrusts itself into the forefront of everyone's preoccupations. Frédéric, who has planned a parallel descent to the physical level in his love for Madame Arnoux, witnesses at close range the sacking of the royal palace and is thereafter, remarks the narrator, 'caught up in the universal madness' (III, i). Hoping to be adopted as a parliamentary candidate after the proclamation of the Republic, he prepares a policy speech. Though it shocks Dambreuse, the extracts quoted express no more than vague and impractical idealism, a liberal democratic call for social justice, with a final appeal to the rich to 'Give! Give!'. His attempt to present it at a *'Club de l'Intelligence'* chaired by Deslauriers' hardline Socialist friend Sénécal is a fiasco, reflecting as critically on the self-seeking of left-wingers and the confusion and ignorance of the common people as on Frédéric's own passive temperament.

The dream of personal self-aggrandisement which helped to fuel Frédéric's political ambition on this occasion recurs later, during his liaison with Madame Dambreuse, and in May 1850 he half-heartedly puts himself forward as a Conservative candidate, having turned against Revolution and even lost faith in the Republic. He shows the self-interest of the *rentier* living on unearned income, the snobbery of the intellectual towards the uneducated masses and a thirst for order which leads him to suggest to Deslauriers that a strong man will have to take charge (III, iii). He seems not to notice that he is echoing the position taken up by Rosanette as early as spring 1848 (III, i); and he subsequently observes with increasing confusion how the extremes of Right and Left are now chanting the same slogans: Force, Authority (III, iv). By the time the strong man emerges, he has lost all interest in politics again; and the two postscript chapters, though chronologically covering almost the whole span of the Second Empire, contain virtually no historical allusions.

Frédéric's general lack of 'commitment', indeed of any real ideological substance, is in part a narrative necessity, allowing him to frequent both sides with equal freedom. But he also symbolises an aspect of Flaubert's general view of the youth of the 1840s. He saw the 'inactive', incompetent or frankly exploitative opponents of the July monarchy as lacking the appropriate skills and vision to win, as well as lacking the personal stature, the dedication to a cause and the sheer energy which had characterised the talented leaders in *Salammbô*. Frédéric's particular combination of inadequacies, in which exploitative egoism plays only a small role, puts him in a clear contrast to Flaubert's picture of the Right as a gang of unscrupulously selfish moneymakers, adept above all at turning coats. A narratorial comment on the Dambreuse salon bluntly indicates:

> Most of the men who were there had served at least four governments, and they would have sold France or the human race to assure the safety of their fortune, to spare themselves an uncomfortable or embarrassing moment, or even out of pure servility, instinctive worship of force. (II, iv)

In fact the general picture of the currents of Opposition is more balanced as well as more detailed than the picture of the Right, within the limits imposed by Flaubert's distrust of all political theories, his detestation of egalitarianism and his tendency to think in broad abstractions such as Justice, Freedom or Beauty; a tendency shared by Frédéric who thus appears in part as a true 'hero' and one moulded in his creator's image. It is also on the Left that Flaubert situates the only completely sincere and authentic positive figure he can bring himself to draw.

Dussardier, the only man of the people in the cast, is one of those simple, direct, quietly noble but doomed individuals whom Flaubert occasionally isolates from a class which as a whole he despises. Educated by Frédéric (an unlikely teacher) he gives himself unsparingly for the cause of social justice and the ideals of 1789. The dashing of his hopes is more tragic than any defeat of Frédéric's superficial commitment, and his suicidal gesture in 1851 both symbolises the end of the Republican dream and sets the shallower attitudes of all the other representative characters in perspective. He is even struck down by his former comrade Sénécal, whose communistic socialism has always been authoritarian, preparing his logical progression to the Napoleonic forces of order. The infinite sympathy which Flaubert had written of to George Sand does not generally stretch to the political figures, where the neutral portrayal of the ideas or principles they express is critically undermined by negative personal traits or the dubious actions in which they are involved. Dussardier, however, is seen in a warm, sympathetic light and repeatedly called, without irony, 'brave', 'honest' or 'poor': a tonality rare in a novel full of sharp-edged demolition of human superficiality or selfishness. He benefits from the novelist's nostalgia for a naïve spontaneity which he himself, as intellectual and artist, has long since lost. He thus becomes a touchstone on the human as well as on the political plane (recalling Justin's role in the apolitical thematics of *Madame Bovary*).

The other social classes represented do not come well out of the comparison, though the working-class origins of Rosanette are not sufficient to make her his moral equal. Only Arnoux, businessman and moderate Republican, shares his qualities of courage, spontaneity and generous warmheartedness. Even his long-suffering wife recognises this one evening in 1848 as they leave the Dambreuse salon, where they have been invited precisely because Arnoux had saved the millionaire's life during street violence:

> He was the only man who had shown any honest feelings during the evening. She felt full of indulgence towards him. (III, iii)

Indulgence is of course the operative word, for Arnoux is also feckless, unfaithful and financially unreliable to the point of criminality. These ambiguities are further illustrated in his scandalous relationship with Frédéric, with whom he cheerfully shares Rosanette and whose obsession with his wife he exploits. There is, reciprocally, something ambiguous in the fatherless youth's quasi-filial attitude to him, a mixture of admiration, envy, jealousy and contempt. Arnoux's Right-wing equivalent, Dambreuse, also shows a paternal interest in Frédéric, and an equivocal attitude to his involvement with *his* wife. But the parallels are there to highlight the contrasts.

Dambreuse's only noble quality is very literally his birth, which, symbolically, had been renounced long ago in the interests of his career. He briefly flirts with the Republic in 1848, but only to save his skin, and he soon finds his natural home in the party of Order. His mouthing of a series of self-contradictory slogans as he shifts telegraphs the novelist's contempt. At least he has no blood on his hands, unlike the newest-rich of the July Monarchy, represented by Roche, who has risen from nothing: he takes his rabid anti-Republicanism, and anger at the personal losses he is suffering, to the extremes, shooting in cold blood a Republican prisoner who refuses to stop calling for bread.

The younger generation of the Right is represented by two contrasted figures. Martinon, from a comfortable middle-class background, works hard, avoids controversy and pursues his climb with discreet efficiency but few scruples: he fits many of Balzac's criteria for success. More likeable, because unmarked by mercenary ambitions, is the inane de Cisy, symbol of the decline of the traditional aristocracy. His muddled thinking and lack of drive echo Frédéric, and despite superficial differences his middle age, like Frédéric's, will be an ironic negation of the life he had aspired to as a young man-about-Paris.

The Left is also represented by two generations. The older are Pellerin, an unsuccessful painter, and Regimbart, a vocal Republican whose political activity seems confined to endless talk in bars. Though their interest in ideas and values neatly opposes them to the philistine Right, their thought is muddled and clichéd, and their achievements meagre. The younger men have more drive and are more directly involved in action. Though self-interested – Dussardier apart – some are credited with a genuine commitment to Republican or Socialist ideals. The personal bitterness of Sénécal is accompanied by serious study of Socialism, an austere lifestyle and a dimension of personal risk. Deslauriers is more cautious and equivocal. It is after all he who advises Frédéric to imitate Rastignac, and he always seeks personal gain, especially of authority. Yet even he on one occasion compromised his professional future to defend his principles (II, i).

In 1848 some of the female characters emerge in the colours of the Republic. Flaubert's misogyny, however, makes it impossible for him to present a remotely balanced view. Rosanette's enthusiasm in February, followed rapidly by revulsion, caricature the male coat-turning; while the historically important strain of militant feminism is devalued by being vested in the figure of La Vatnaz, procuress and embezzler. The total failure of the Second Republic meant that Flaubert did not have to strain his own profound pessimism by including any 'winners' on the Left. It is true that alongside Martinon his love of structural parallels placed the successful Hussonnet, who ends up a powerful figure in charge of the theatres and the press; but his 'commitment', even in his 'radical' days, had always cynically been to building his career.

Hussonnet is also significant as the only writer in a book which includes a substantial treatment of the Arts in the 1840s. The fact that he mostly practises the non-art of journalism is symptomatic not only of the way Flaubert now angles his treatment away from literature towards the plastic and performing arts (in contrast to the first *Education*) but also of the negative image he now presents of all artistic practice at the time. Satirical emphasis is laid on various common features, which Flaubert hated or despised. Among these are: 'industrial art', Arnoux's slogan in his entrepreneurial roles; commitment, in the political posturings of Pellerin and the actor Delmar in 1848; and, mostly in other facets of Pellerin, excessive theorising at the expense of creation, imitation of the masters, vulgar popularisation. Flaubert shares some of the blame out evenly between weaknesses in the creators and external pressures, especially those of the market place. Thus Pellerin is first seen compromising his ideals in order to earn his living from Arnoux's commissions, and he ends in the 1860s a servant of the newfangled technology, photography. Yet the dice are always loaded, for the completed artworks described in the novel – Pellerin's paintings, Arnoux's prints, pots and religious ornaments, Delmar's performances – are aesthetic failures; though the novelist does seem to respect the way Arnoux and Pellerin, by certain efforts to pursue an elusive perfection of form, dimly resemble himself.

The opening pages of the novel wrongly suggest that literature too will have a considerable part to play; and the reasons why this theme peters out shed more light on Flaubert's negative diagnosis of the arts in general. Frédéric's schoolboy dream echoes that of his creator: 'he had ambitions to be one day France's Walter Scott' (I, ii). At eighteen he has turned to confessional poetry: 'he esteemed passion above all'. The subjective strain, abhorrent to the mature Flaubert, continues in Frédéric's attempt to write a novel in which he imagines the unlikely conquest of Madame Arnoux in an equally unrealistic Venice (I, iii). Things grow worse when Frédéric turns to painting for the totally selfish reasons that it might draw him nearer to Madame Arnoux and impress her. This failure to take the creative act seriously for itself mars a later attempt to write, when he is oscillating between her and Rosanette:

> In the middle of his work, often the face of one or other woman passed before him; he struggled against the desire to see her, quickly gave way (. . .) (II, ii)

Only once does Frédéric's recourse to artistic creation meet with Flaubert's approval. It is during a painful period of frustration and despair over the indifference of Madame Arnoux:

> (. . .) to distract himself from his calamitous passion, adopting the first subject which presented itself, he determined to compose a *History of the Renaissance* (. . .) Little by little the serenity of the work calmed him down. By plunging into the personalities of other people, he forgot his own personality: it is perhaps the only way of not suffering from it. (II, iii)

– Flaubert himself making a fleeting appearance in the generalising present tense of the final clause. Apart from sentimentality and self-regard, dilettantism is Frédéric's major weakness as a budding artist, for he is just as likely to be 'inspired' by Madame Arnoux to consider a career in the professions or politics (e.g. in I, v, II, ii, III, i, iii) as in the arts: a proof *a contrario* of the dictum of Buffon which Flaubert had made his own: 'Talent is only a long patience'. Frédéric, like all the other artist-figures, is totally lacking in this quality. Hence the novel, though it may have in Dussardier its Justin, has no figure to equal Dr Larivière.

The novel's unremitting picture of mediocrity and self-seeking, rounded off by a litany of failures – a picture which has modern

critics writing of its 'nihilism' – was probably a cause of early
reviewers' complaints about its shapelessness. It is not structured
in the way Balzac or Stendhal had built their 'novels of education',
round a dynamic hero interacting positively and fruitfully with his
world, hence creating a strong plot and high tension in the reader.
Indeed in 1879 a 'new novelist' of the next generation, Emile
Zola, turned traditional criteria upside down by calling the work
a masterpiece and a model to young writers precisely because it
presented life in a relentlessly ordinary and shapeless way, and
because Flaubert refused to exaggerate for poetic effect. Flaubert
expressed delight at the article (VIII, 329); though it is difficult
to believe that he was entirely satisfied with Zola's approach. In
offering his vibrant testimony to the truth of the novel's image of
individual and society, Zola made only token allusions to technique
and style, while Flaubert's creative efforts had been evenly divided,
his aim an intimate fusion of 'truth' and 'beauty'.

Like his earlier novels, *L'Education Sentimentale* is through-composed
for a total effect. Chance, despite its major function in the lives of the
characters, plays no part in the composition. Apparent heterogeneity
and disorder yield on close examination to a strong sense of pattern.
Some examples have been discussed already. More generally, the
private destinies of the fictional characters both mirror, and in
Flaubert's view explain, the historical fate of France. The country
toys with the idea of a fair and just Republic which, when it comes,
is as sickly and short-lived as Frédéric's illegitimate son. Only a
Dussardier will fight to preserve it, and he does so in a state
of increasing confusion, then despair. Self-interest is everywhere
stronger than the selfless ideals of 1789, as Frédéric finds when
he questions the man-in-the-street on December 3rd, 1851: neither
bourgeois nor worker will fight to defend the Republic against
Napoleon (III, v).

The leitmotivs of fusion and confusion which mark the political
domain between 1848 and 1851 are precisely echoed not only in
the shifts of Frédéric's own attitude, but also in his love-life. Hence
in the same salon where Arnoux argues politics with Dambreuse
and Roche, three of Frédéric's women are assembled to discuss
the fourth. The absentee, Rosanette, is typical of the structural
and thematic interrelations. She has been the subject of a painting by Pellerin; has aspired to hold a political salon; while the
theme of prostitution which she quite literally embodies underlies

the novelist's vision of all the social groups he describes: artists, businessmen, politicians, repeatedly prostitute themselves or their values for money or power.

Flaubert's method is, as ever, elliptical and allusive, depending on juxtaposition rather than overt commentary to make its points. Despite the author's decision to have 'no metaphors', the language and style lose nothing of their denseness of meaning, for the whole novel is turned into a forest of symbols. Thus the setting of the opening scene – a river-boat – discreetly prepares the drifting of Frédéric, who allows himself to be led where others take him. It also indicates a certain detachment from his surroundings, as here from the river banks gliding by: an initial rootlessness and aimlessness which love, friendship, ideals, vocations, will never manage to counteract. Hence at the end of the book the brief summary of Frédéric's life after 1851 begins with expanded echoes of the opening motifs:

> He travelled.
> He experienced the melancholy of passenger ships, cold awaken-
> ings under canvas, the dizziness caused by landscapes and ruins,
> the bitterness of interrupted friendships. (III, vi)

There are echoes, too, of Flaubert's own stance (and precise ex- periences) after his attack of 1844. But he had always insisted on his deliberate, conscious adoption of an attitude of detachment, and justified it in terms of the special needs of the artist. Frédéric, as we have just seen, has no such excuse. Since Henry James, Anglo-Saxon critics have been uncomfortable with such an unheroic protagonist. But of course Frédéric's views do not embody Flaubert's values, which emerge from the total experience of the work. The reader, watching Frédéric watching, is in a position to judge the quality of his eyesight. Thus a striking feature of the many deliberately fragmentary subplots is the way the reader can examine and interpret evidence which Frédéric does no more than glimpse and record. As usual, Flaubert's narrative techniques allow him to be true to the often conflicting requirements of his own standpoint, which insists on shaping the work of art yet is reluctant to shape too firmly and clearly the image of man and society it contains. Indeed, with time that image has to reflect a Flaubert even more certain of uncertainties and decided on indecisiveness. If the reader is placed, finally, in the position of 'God', as Flaubert wishes, it is a 'God' who reflects Flaubert's inability to make up his mind on the religious question, too.

This very combination of uncertainties will run as a key theme through the final works of fiction, as Flaubert at last puts aside his fascination with Romantic love to concentrate on illustrating, with many of the skills acquired since 1850, those broad general questions of life and death which had dominated the writing of his teens and twenties.

7

Trois Contes

Although Flaubert occasionally nurtured projects for short fictional works – in particular for an Oriental tale – he wrote none for some thirty years after his youthful experiments. Only frustration with the slow progress made on *Bouvard et Pécuchet* drove him back to the form in the autumn of 1875, as an exercise in style, a relaxing therapy and a way of proving that he had not lost the capacity to write. On holiday in Brittany he began a *conte* retelling the life of St Julian the Hospitaller (originally planned in 1856). Its brevity and the legendary quality of the subject had no effect on his method. He made no attempt to finish his text from his memory and imagination while on holiday: he must first consult the sources, examine his dossiers on the background. By the time he completed the text, in February 1876, he had planned two more: the life of a servant woman in Normandy, spanning the nineteenth century (*Un Coeur Simple*) and the last day of John the Baptist (*Hérodias*). Completed by February 1877, the three stories were published together as, simply, *Trois Contes*, in April.

Not only did this volume represent a new formal departure, after a series of long and complex novels, it seemed to aim at the widest possible variety within the short stories' compass: in setting (biblical, medieval, modern), in timescale (from twenty-four hours to seventy years) and in structure (from the single strand of a biography to the multiple interrelation of a dozen significant characters). The collection also neatly summarises Flaubert's three great literary preoccupations: modern France, hagiography, and the ancient history of the Mediterranean civilisations. But in each case the story marks a new departure. The modern work focuses for the first time on a plebeian protagonist; the saint's legend is set in medieval Europe, while the ancient history is that of Palestine at the time of Christ.

Despite this wide variety, the stories' themes have much in common, and it is tempting to see them almost as a single work illustrating three main phases in the history of Christianity. The origins are treated in John's prophecy; *La Légende de St Julien l'Hospitalier* evokes a golden age of belief and mystery, of God's power active in the world; while the naïve faith of the servant Félicité, set against the empty outward show and ritual of modern Catholicism, represents a late stage of decline and decay, which is given greater emphasis by appearing first in the volume. Looked at in another way, the great difference in period between the stories is less important than the close similarities between three central characters, who are all in their different ways martyrs and saints. Certainly one of their great merits, in Flaubert's eyes, must have been their total detachment from the middle-class world of *Bouvard et Pécuchet* and its fundamental mediocrity. The stories, indeed, contain none of the comic tonality of the bourgeois novels.

Hérodias, curiously, is the story least concerned with the theme of sainthood. Flaubert himself, commenting in 1876 that he was writing a lot about saints, insisted that at least his 'John the Baptist' would not be an edifying tale: his main themes were race and politics (VII, 309). As his title indicates, the story does not concentrate either on the figure of Christ (though the brief mention, by invoking miracles, links this text to the other two) or that of John, who is heard more in his role of angry, Jewish prophet of Israel's doom than as the definitive voice announcing the coming Messiah. The body of the story contains a remarkable compression of the politics, passions and ambitions in conflict in Palestine around the time of Christ's preaching, the secular background to the beginnings of Christianity, for which Flaubert leaned heavily on Greek and Roman historians. His reader, more familiar with the Gospel narrative, thus gains an entirely new perspective on the events. At the same time, he has the sense that lesser conflicts occupy centre stage: the major issue, historically, the coming of Christ, being kept in the wings like the Punic Wars in *Salammbô*.

This effect of extratextual perspective is weakened, for the modern reader of *Hérodias*, by the fact that history since 1877 has assured a painful relevance for Flaubert's picture of the region as a battlefield of sectional, racial and religious interests exacerbated by the involvement of foreign superpowers. Many readers find that the sheer complexity of the political and ideological issues finally defeats

Flaubert's art in the limited compass of the 'tale'. Certainly he has room for only the briefest of signposts to situate the numerous conflicts symbolically brought together, at considerable cost to strict chronological accuracy, on a single day in Herod's palace at Machaerous. It may, however, be argued that the sense of obscurity and confusion created is probably just the effect that the ever sceptical Flaubert sought in the first place.

Apart from this suggestive and thought-provoking historical perspective, Flaubert also adds to the bald Gospel narrative the dimension of psychology and motivation, painting Herod as fearful and mediocre, Hérodias as ambitious, strong-willed and passionate, driven not only by political expediency but also the shame and insecurity of being Herod's queen by a marriage of dubious legality. Her plan, hidden like many of the stratagems in *Salammbô*, can be guessed at by the reader, who picks up clues which Herod, self-absorbed and blind as Frédéric Moreau, fails to understand. Indeed the story is full of characteristic features of Flaubert's vision of human nature. The great and powerful are devalued systematically. Vitellius, the Roman governor feared by Herod, trembles for his own job, which depends on the Emperor's perverted interest in his son, who is no Adonis but a fat adolescent, a compulsive eater (one of Flaubert's favourite devices for showing up the animality of man). Any crowd is implicitly denigrated, from the common people to a clutch of high-ranking officials. Female sexuality is a redoubtable destabiliser; while marriage is unsuccessful, entered for selfish reasons and disappointing even those.

The characteristic 'apparition' of the ideal woman is reduced to an erotic impulse, though it still results in Herod, on contemplating Salome, surrendering his independence, like Charles, Mâtho and Frédéric before him. The metaphysical dimension is presented ambiguously, through a clash of opinions. A full-scale argument about resurrection – again accompanied by a feast – ends inconclusively; Phanuel's astrologically-inspired prophecy is juxtaposed to the divinely-inspired words of John (carefully 'distanced' by being saddled with the barbarously unfamiliar name Iaokanann). The executioner's claim to have seen an angel protecting John is contradicted by the pragmatic Romans, who not only saw, but killed, 'a Jewish captain', making any possible miracle a question of point of view, as will happen with Félicité's deathbed religious vision. But whereas the executioner eventually carries out his task,

Phanuel, in the final lines of the story, leaves his post and sets off 'towards Galilee', with John's followers, prefiguring the faith of the apostles, who leave everything to follow Jesus.

The theme of language itself is treated no less ambiguously. Communication is frequently a problem for the characters, whether in the context of allusive and obscure prophecies or of interlocutors speaking through interpreters. But there are hints of the power of the word. It is John's word, 'this force more pernicious than the sword', that drives Hérodias to fury; echoing Flaubert's conviction that the hostility of censorship, authority, society or critics to some writers reflected a similar fear of the truth-telling power of their language.

Flaubert certainly displayed his own technical powers, fusing erudition with spectacle and sometimes disturbing psychology, as he had in *Salammbô*. His topographic descriptions are again evocative and symbolic, while in the rather gratuitous inventory of Herod's secret armoury he seems to be unleashing the forces of his own unconscious, first in a spiral of sadism inspired by the weaponry, then in a mysterious description of the king's prized horses, which some critics have interpreted as projections of the novelist's own repressed energy and violence.[30]

The interplay of characters' words and silences, prominent here, recurs in the other tales, and has perhaps contributed to a whole school of interpretation which seeks to 'read' the saint figures as projections of Flaubert's severe and ascetic concept of how the artist should relate to himself and to others.[31] The analogy cannot be denied; but it should not be forgotten that as in all the other analogies between Flaubert and his main characters, there remains the central difference that none of the characters is a creative artist. Even Bouvard and Pécuchet, though they wield pens, will get no farther than copying, shoring up fragments, not constructing a work, and doing it for themselves, not for others.

If Flaubert's aim was to put religion in a secondary place in *Hérodias*, he could hardly do the same with the life of St Julian. However, his approach to the legend resembles his use of the Gospels in that he grafts on additions and explanations, bringing to bear his erudition, his concept of human nature and his sceptical view of religious interpretations of the world. He adds first a great deal of colour, notably in descriptions of costumes, buildings and hunting scenes, though avoiding the precise localisation which is such a feature of *Hérodias*. Secondly he develops the personality of Julien to help explain events. Thirdly, he redraws the lines which in the legend restrict the field of divine intervention. Given the long timespan, he is able to adopt some of the techniques of the novels to fix the psychology.

Julien's mother and father are briefly characterised as representatives of the complementary religious and military attitudes to life of the Middle Ages, with Julien inheriting something from each. Education develops both innate traits, and the narrative structure itself repeatedly underlines their interrelations: Julien's first experience of killing takes place in Church. The doctor's son then carefully traces the escalation of this syndrome and of the accompanying emotional responses. Julien's father innocently conspires by having him equipped and taught to hunt. But the fantasy of legend is not forgotten: the whole animal kingdom is exposed to Julien's bloodlust, which culminates in a solitary expedition of hallucinatory destructiveness.

The often hyperbolic feelings and desires of Flaubert's modern, 'realistic' characters may be carried into action in the legend. When a magic stag resists his weapons long enough to deliver a terrible curse-cum-prophecy that he will kill his parents, it is explicitly related to his given character as a 'savage heart'. Julien, weighed down by this, falls ill, communicating his secret to no-one, partly because he is not sure that he would be incapable of such a deed, especially if the Devil took a hand. The typical Flaubertian oscillation between two possible responsibilities, that of the human individual and that of a higher power, will continue throughout the text. Thus his parents and the castle priest between them help to generate the circumstances where unintentionally, but responding to the promptings of his 'savage heart', he almost fulfils the prophecy. Julien's parents have been given different prophecies about his future, his mother being told categorically that he will be a saint, his father more confusingly hearing:

Ah! ah! your son! . . . much blood! . . . much glory! . . . always happy! . . . the family of an emperor! (I)

Although he flees his parents' castle and lands, he cannot escape his personality, and his new career as a soldier combines his savage heart with a desire to escape the curse by dying in battle; to which

is added a new feature, the defence of what is right. Winning the
hand of a Princess whose Oriental milieu is one of Flaubert's devices
for avoiding too 'local' a colour, Julien finds himself back at peace,
able to listen again to the temptations of his nature and the regret
for his lost parents. His wife tries to overcome his sadness, urging
him to return to hunting. Though he reveals the prophecy, she
argues it away. But when Julien does succumb, it is not to the lure
of her arguments, but to mysteriously attractive shapes and sounds
of animals. This time he pursues a sequence of predator animals,
neither harming, nor being harmed by them. Their vengeance, like
the menace of the magic stag, will be indirect, for they merely
build up his frustrated bloodlust so that when he returns home to
find a male head on his wife's pillow in the darkness his response
will be swift and violent. Like the rest of the story, the scene is a
delicate balance of modern realism – in the attendant circumstances
– legendary magic and religious mystery, with a cruelly ironic
overall effect.

Julien's parents, with good reason to believe that the prophecies
made to them are being realised, are killed as they peacefully await
his return. It is tempting to see the role of Julien's wife as a misplaced
example of Flaubert's misogyny. Certainly she influences events no
less than three times, and Flaubert's most striking deviation from
his medieval sources is to send Julien out alone on his penitential
road, rejecting the positive view of marriage presented by the legend,
where the wife shares and comforts. But to say, as Duckworth does,[32]
that 'it is because he cannot forgive her that he goes off alone', is to
ignore the text. For while the legends seem to dissociate entirely the
early phases of Julien's life from any divine intervention, Flaubert's
Julien exculpates his wife precisely by invoking God's role. The
narrator reports his words:

> She had obeyed the will of God in causing his crime and must pray
> for his soul, since from this day on he no longer existed. (II)

Julien then begins a second purgatory on earth, separated from
his fellow-men by his crime. The paradox of Julien's attitude is
neatly summed up:

> He did not revolt against God who had inflicted this action
> upon him, and yet he despaired at having committed it. (III)

Flaubert does not tell us whether it is from God that 'the idea came to him to use his life in the service of others'. The noble Julien becomes a servant, struggling at thankless tasks like Félicité. The relentless realism of these paragraphs gives way gradually to the marvellous, which will dominate the final episode. First comes a voice, unbelievably audible through a storm and 'with the intonation of a church bell', then the waters are instantaneously calmed. Yet the reader loses contact neither with concrete reality in all its ugliness (the caller is a leper), nor with the evolution of Julien's character. He is now all tenderness in the face of danger or horror, and his total forgetfulness of self has its reward, for he is at last carried skywards, the miracle happening this time in full view of the reader. But the text does not end on this paragraph of full-blown lyricism. Flaubert, who had already introduced the word *Legend* into the title of his story, distances himself twice more with a last sentence which brings the reader back to a modern perspective and presents the author as no more than a translator:

> And that is the story of St Julian the Hospitaller, more or less as it is found on a stained glass window in a church near my home. (III)

The text had, of course, made no real effort to respect precisely the nature and limitations of either the medieval story or the purely visual medium of the glass. Indeed, planning a later edition, Flaubert tried to persuade his publisher to include a reproduction of Rouen's St Julian window; not as an illustration – he abhorred illustrations of literary texts – but as a document:

> Comparing the image to the text, people would have said: 'I can't understand it. How did he get this from that?' (VIII, 207)

The mystificatory intent is not confined to this trick. Flaubert in the story itself walks one of his customary 'tightropes', this time between the past and the present. He seeks to satisfy both the modern demand for verisimilitude and human motivations, and the medieval belief in mystery, in the power of the divinity, and in that coexistence of the ordinary and the marvellous which is such a feature of its thought as of its visual arts.

Yet while providing both a context and motivations, he is careful not to conclude, and leaves the story doubly open-ended.

The final 'cutaway' refuses to endorse the miraculous, while the whole complex account leaves unresolved the dialectic of individual responsibility v. divinely controlled determinism. Unlike his sources, Flaubert offers no explicit reason why Christ comes to save Julien, so that his God, finally, moves in a more mysterious way than that of medieval hagiographers. It has always been the artist's privilege to refuse to answer the questions he puts. Flaubert wrote in 1879:

> The people who surprise me are not those who try to explain the incomprehensible, but those who think they have found the explanation, those who have 'le bon Dieu' (or 'le non Dieu') in their pocket. Yes indeed! any dogmatism exasperates me. In a word, materialism and spiritualism seem to me to be two impertinences. (VIII, 327)

In his final revision of *La Tentation*, in 1872, he had made substantial changes both to the manner and to the structure of his drama of the testing of faith. One of the most striking involved displacing to the final pages the monologue in which Antoine, watching the extraordinary diversity of life-forms, feels the temptation to fuse with matter. In its new position, the context is the post-Darwinian sense of how life began. But just when the reader expects Antoine to declare himself a scientific materialist who has no need of God to explain the world, there comes a miraculous vision of the face of Christ in the sun which is rising to end Antoine's long night, and the final stage direction:

> Antoine crosses himself and begins his prayers again.

Though silent, this ending may well seem more affirmative than, in the earlier versions, the sounds of Antoine's desperate prayers intercut with the scornful laughter of the Devil. Yet no attempt is made to reconcile the successive postures of Antoine. 'The good thing about theatre', Flaubert had written many years before, 'is that it annuls the author' (III, 61). So, to a very large extent, did the short story, as practised in this volume.

                                    *

With *Un Coeur Simple* there is no game of hide-and-seek between ancient sources and modern interpretations. The story is entirely Flaubert's, indeed intimately so, for it is steeped in his own memories of the region in which it is set, and uses for partial model Julie, an old family servant who was still alive in the 1870s, growing blind and infirm. Yet the story's structure contains a curious echo of the way the other two retell and expand a pre-existing narrative.

It begins with a brief, schematic outline of Félicité's adult life, seen from the outside, which is then elaborated in greater detail. The first chapter presents the ideal servant, reliable, hardworking, conscientious, undemanding. As she grows old in the job, she becomes completely dehumanised, and the chapter ends with this strong image:

> ... she seemed to be a woman made of wood functioning in an automatic way.

The other chapters, going beyond this appearance, demolish the implications of the image. Though a creature of limited intelligence, driven by basic instincts, Félicité is never a woman of wood. The sufferings to which her real sensibility will repeatedly expose her, while recalling the sadistic undercurrent present in the two other tales, seem mainly to illustrate Flaubert's own warnings, throughout his correspondence, of the danger one runs by allowing oneself to have feelings. Sign of superiority over the bourgeois, it is also one's Achilles heel. The greater importance of the theme of feeling here, compared with the other tales, is stressed in Flaubert's own comments on it. He insisted that his aim this time was not to be cold and inhuman, but to appear 'a sensitive man' (VII, 331), and to generate pity in his readers for Félicité (VII, 307).

Chapter II thus announces itself the story of her love and observes from the outside the feeling as it is transferred from an unworthy youth who leaves her in the lurch to the children of her mistress and thence to a long-lost nephew. All take her for granted, and though active and surrounded by colour and life, Félicité is already basically alone, like the saints in the other tales. In Chapter III, the reader is installed inside Félicité's consciousness and the theme of religion is grafted onto that of feeling. The choice of her viewpoint allows the author to conceal narratorial opinions on the validity both of what she is taught and what she makes of it, though he has no difficulty in indicating such opinions by his customary tactics of juxtaposition or *reductio ad absurdum*, to which he is able to add the naïve questions of Félicité herself, briefly adopting the role of *Candide* (or Bouvard or Pécuchet).

The description of Virginie's first communion, however, reminds us that for Flaubert the object of a feeling matters less than the intensity and authenticity of the feeling itself. Félicité is never closer to her middle-class predecessors in his fiction than when she is identifying intensely with the communion of Virginie, never, that is, except when experiencing a typical disappointment with the concrete reality of her own communion the next day. In this brief story, Flaubert has almost achieved his goal of narratorial non-intervention; but one of the two explicit generalisations accompanies Félicité's identification with Virginie, which is attributed to 'the imagination that true feelings of tenderness bring'. The same imagination is stirred later by her unworthy and unappreciative nephew Victor, to whom she transfers her tenderness when Virginie has been sent off to school.

Her 'simple heart', in contrast to Julien's, will always be a tender one. In other ways there are curious parallels between the two, scaled down to fit Félicité's modest social reality. Her courage, for example, is shown in the face of the somewhat domestic challenge of a bull. She makes, on foot, several painful journeys which, pilgrimages of affection in intent, become Calvaries in miniature as she suffers all kinds of disappointments and indignities. Ironies abound in them, as when she commends the departing Victor to God, only for him to die some time later in the West Indies. Soon after, Virginie, seeming to improve in health, has a sudden relapse and dies. Félicité watches the body, like Flaubert with his sister or Le Poittevin, or Charles with Emma; and the narrator's second aside pinpoints the nature of the mysterious or miraculous dimension in this modern story:

> She kissed (Virginie's eyes) several times; and would not have felt any great surprise if Virginie had opened them again; for such souls the supernatural is quite simple. (III)

When Félicité's tenderness broadens to embrace a wider world than her 'family', the effect is almost to parody *St Julien*: her final object of devotion, le père Colmiche, is more or less an outcast, suffering notably from a prominent tumour on his arm. But there is an extra episode in Félicité's life, after her 'leper'. A parrot gradually becomes the focus first of her emotional, then of her religious preoccupations. The few joys and many sufferings of Félicité's earlier life are repeated with the usual ironic twists. Thus one of the parrot's escapades, by involving her in a long hunt, undermines her robust health; while the desire to keep it, after its death, precipitates the most brutally painful of her pilgrimages to Honfleur.

The gradual fusion of the parrot with her image of the Holy Spirit is as carefully plotted and motivated as the development of St Julian's bloodlust or his progress to selflessness. Félicité has never had much communication with others, and old age and deafness intensify this typical Flaubertian situation. It is noticeable that even her brief communion in grief and memory with her mistress, the momentary abolition of so many barriers, is wordless:

> they embraced, satisfying their suffering in a kiss which made them equal. (III)

The stripping down of a life to its bare essentials had, in the cases of John and Julien, given them lucidity and heroic stature in the face of a cruel world. The modern parallels are unheroic, involving the thoughtless indifference of Madame Aubin's son and daughter-in-law (the sale of furniture, the deterioration of the fabric of the house) and Félicité's own realistically-portrayed decline into invalidity, some senile mental confusion, blindness and finally pneumonia. The pathos of the situation is underlined by repeated references to her thoughts and feelings as well as by external description. The last scene rhythms together the solemnity and spectacle of the Corpus Christi procession with Félicité's death throes, alternating poetry and medical realism until in the final lines it is the realism which gives way to the poetry, transferred now to the evocation of Félicité as she dies content and confident in her simple belief:

> Her lips were smiling. The movements of her heart slowed one by one, each more vague, more gentle, like a spring drying up, like an echo disappearing; and, when she breathed out her last breath, she thought she saw, in the heavens as they opened, a huge parrot, gliding over her head. (V)

There is no miracle, only an individual vision, and it is tempting to detach the parrot from its place in Félicité's mental processes and see it as another parodic distortion of the religious theme. But the poetic text is not, this time, undercut by a deliberate distancing device. On the contrary, Flaubert is trying to draw his reader in, to identify with the 'simple' character and her perspective: hence the careful rhythms, the brief similes, creating an atmosphere of peace so different from the deaths of Emma or Salammbô. This of course does not mean that Flaubert shares Félicité's faith, though he may well envy its way of resolving the problem of living – and dying – in a cruel, unfeeling and even absurd world.

*

Since Edgar Allan Poe's early essays on the short story, the genre has frequently been compared more to lyric poetry than to the longer narrative forms. It is often argued that to succeed, it must suggest, opening up new perspectives as it resonates in the reader's mind. Though he was neither a theoretician of the form nor an assiduous practitioner of it, Flaubert did in *Trois Contes* produce texts of concentrated power and extraordinary suggestivity. The stories have occasional weak points, in the clarity of narration, of continuity or even of style. But their ambiguous, enigmatic quality is on the whole deliberate, and an important factor in the hold they have taken on generations of readers, who will no doubt continue to disagree about their basic meaning.[33] At once Romantic and Realist, objective in their narrative techniques yet deeply personal in their links to Flaubert's most abiding intellectual preoccupations and deepest-rooted impulses, they manage to incarnate many of the qualities of his established art as a novelist and show him mastering, in late middle age, the skills required of a demanding new literary form.

8
Bouvard et Pécuchet

Flaubert probably found the inspiration for the narrative framework of his last, unfinished and most ambitious novel in an unpretentious comic tale by one B. Maurice, *Les Deux Greffiers* (The two court clerks). Maurice's heroes, on retirement, move to the country where, after various unsuccessful attempts to fill the long hours with hobbies, they return to copying just in time to save their sanity and their friendship. In 1863 Flaubert sketched a variation, in which the pastimes would be replaced by attempts at serious study. He took up the plan again in 1872, on completing his final version of *La Tentation*; indeed he presented it as a modern and comic counterpart to that work, a review of all contemporary ideas (Sup. III, 39-40). He wrote to a friend:

> It's the story of these two chaps who copy a kind of critical encyclopaedia made farcical. (VI, 402)

The copying – his original title was *Les Deux Copistes* – was to be the final episode in an odyssey through many domains of science, arts and thought. Though he considered the general idea excellent, he also thought himself slightly mad to undertake the massive documentary reading programme it required. Scholars estimate that he may not have exaggerated his later claim to have read 1500 volumes (VIII, 355-6). Certainly two years of study and planning went by before he began on the text of Chapter I, and of course he abandoned the writing altogether for eighteen months to compose *Trois Contes*. His sudden death interrupted work on the text of Chapter X. Published soon afterwards, with only the sketchiest indication of how the book would have continued, the novel was for a long time treated as an enigma. As we shall see, the more recent publication of the scenarios and some of the dossiers has hardly solved all the problems of interpretation.[34]

It is clear from letters that Flaubert saw the work as primarily a philosophical tale. Friends vainly tried to persuade him to keep it short, like Voltaire's masterpieces in the form, especially *Candide*, which Flaubert greatly admired, and which also concludes with a reasoned return from ambitious speculation to everyday tasks. He insisted that length and detail were necessary to make it 'serious', even 'frightening' (VII, 178). He refused the option of fantasy offered by Voltaire, and worked as hard on the authenticity of setting and characterisation as of the ideas treated. As a result, the novel brings together for the first time explicitly the realistic fiction-making and the philosophically-reflective sides of his writing. It resembles *Madame Bovary* in its choice of a modern Normandy setting and mediocre middle-class characters, but echoes *La Tentation* in that the protagonists' insatiable curiosity leads them to ask some fundamental questions about the world, man and God. As to the tone and manner, Flaubert repeatedly declared his intention of writing an angry book against human stupidity (*la bêtise*); angry but also comic.

The opening chapter fuses very well these intentions. It presents in some detail Bouvard and Pécuchet, copyists in different Paris offices, who meet by chance. There is instant mutual attraction, developing into the most solid and harmonious example of male bonding in Flaubert, an apotheosis of his ideal of friendship between bachelors; yet given a comic turn by their relatively advanced age, which is that of Frédéric and Deslauriers at the *end* of their story. Though the copyists have features in common, the attraction is mainly that of complementary opposites. Bouvard, who has been briefly married, is plump, earthy, a joker, pragmatic and sceptical. Pécuchet, a virgin bachelor, is lean, rather timid, studious, unworldly and eager for certitudes. They subtly influence each other, notably in developing a common taste for knowledge and for a wider experience of the world. Curiosity expands their intelligence, bringing sufferings, for they now chafe at the limited horizons imposed by their office work, feeling wounded in their new-found self-esteem. Their shared encyclopaedic urge has often been compared to Flaubert's own; while in their temperamental differences they repeat the novelist's perception of himself as a double personality: Pécuchet aspires always to the ideal, while Bouvard is happy in the real, in 'the animalities of man'.

The same pages briefly introduce a cross-section of the many areas the novel will explore later, from politics, sex and religions to fossils and plants. The decision to put an equal pair of protagonists at the centre of the narrative structure offers technical and presentational advantages, both for varying the introduction of new themes and for illuminating contrasts and contradictions. The tone is predominantly comic, even grotesque, as their naïvety (the French word *candide* means naïve) and lack of culture are complaisantly illustrated; they also mouth received ideas and are shown to be physically clumsy and incompetent in practicalities. Yet like Emma Bovary they possess positive qualities: the capacity for affection, the thirst for something better than a humdrum workaday existence, and tremendous energy and resilience. They are also, like Charles, devoid of such negative traits as self-seeking ambition and lust for wealth or power.

Though their friendship will be marked by many an argument, they will never exploit each other, as Flaubert's earlier bachelor pairs had done. These positive qualities are all brought into relief when Bouvard inherits a small fortune and, in accordance with received ideas, they retire to the country. The leading personalities of Chavignolles are shown to be devoid of energy, intellectual curiosity, disinterest or affection, and relations with them will be sporadic, each new contact ending in disagreement and antagonism.

The reader's dominant impression is at first of a comic duo. For perhaps half the novel they function mainly as instruments for the farcical presentation of lower middle-class scientific pretentions. Being men of the nineteenth century, they combine worship of the printed word with the determination to try things out for themselves. Being Flaubert characters, they fail dismally to grasp the principles of the pure sciences or to achieve satisfactory results in the applied. There are diverse reasons for this. As well as lacking intelligence and dexterity, they lack method and critical judgement, plunging into subjects via the first books they lay hands on (often provided by a shadowy and hardly better-qualified friend), then hastening to apply their sketchy and ill-digested knowledge.

They also lack persistence; as with Emma or Frédéric, new interests flare up briefly, to die down in the face of difficulties or with the mere passage of time. Confirmed believers in received ideas, they seek precise parameters and neat, fixed definitions. They abandon physiology as 'the romance of medicine' because it fails to oblige (III); and find it 'sad' that history will never be 'fixed' once and for all (IV). Yet their own approach is contradictorily haphazard, symbolised by the mishmash of styles and periods they incorporate into their formal garden (II). If the novel is, as Flaubert claimed, an illustration of 'the absence of method in science' (VIII, 366), it seems to apply rather to the practice of incompetent amateurs than to the professionals; especially as chance not infrequently contributes to their failure. However, with time the pair's own scepticism at the end of each experiment (and there will be over thirty in all) is contagious; and they begin to highlight the contradictions or absurdities in the authorities they have consulted. They sense the resistance of the subject-matter itself, be it the complexity of the human body or the sheer size and inaccessibility of the earth's crust. They will never achieve the smug self-confidence of Monsieur Homais or the inhabitants of Chavignolles.

The lesson Bouvard and Pécuchet repeatedly draw clearly has the approval of their sceptical 'conclusion'-hating creator, for all the fun he pokes at them. Yet with each branch of knowledge they have to learn it all over again, illustrating his oft-expressed opinion that there is something immovable about stupidity. After acquitting themselves well in archaeological debate with the priest (III), they are as gullible as ever while collecting historical relics (IV). Real changes in their perspicacity seem to owe less to any evolution planned by the novelist – there is no proper 'intellectual education' – than to accidental convergences of their viewpoint with that of Flaubert himself. Thus, studying literature (V), they briskly identify the weaknesses Flaubert found in historical fiction and drama, Sir Walter Scott, Balzac or the discursive comic novel ('the author effaces his work by displaying his personality in it'). But they still read indiscriminately, and their efforts at acting or writing are as comic as anything in *L'Education Sentimentale*.

Yet when they consider aesthetic theory they astutely pinpoint the incoherences both of the authorities and of the central concept. The naturally sceptical Bouvard takes this in his stride, but Pécuchet, thirsting for certitudes, makes himself ill. The reader may smile at aesthetics-induced jaundice, but it marks a stage towards greater seriousness in the couple's reactions to their – or their subjects' – failures.

Though subtly varying his presentations to give them an air of spontaneity, Flaubert not only repeats the underlying pattern of enthusiasm, trial, defeat and sceptical retreat; he also leads his heroes through the applied and pure sciences, then the arts, to the human sciences, reaching politics (VI). This is the only episode rooted in precise historical events; elsewhere the chronology is vague and incoherent, perhaps through quasi-Voltairean indifference, perhaps in an attempt to gloss over the advancing age of the energetic protagonists. The context for their political education is the period 1848 to 1851. Though the perspective is provincial, Flaubert's implicit attitude is that of *L'Education Sentimentale*. His heroes, whose originality and enterprise have given them a reputation for radicalism, gradually become isolated as the Republican spirit peters out. Reaction sets in and Napoleon even wins the popular vote. Perspicacious as their creator again, they watch the coat-turning élite and marvel at the prompt submission of the lower classes.

Unlike Frédéric, they are profoundly depressed by the *coup d'état*, and for a time lose their enviable resilience, so Flaubert engineers a romantic interlude (VII). 'Romantic' is hardly the right word for love in this novel where, displaced to a secondary role for the first time, it is even there only a sexual, social and economic, not emotional and imaginative, experience. The two men lust, the females exploit, Bouvard narrowly saves his farm from the cupidity of a widow, Pécuchet catches syphilis. Cured – in both senses – they reaffirm their bachelor friendship and resume study.

A new sequence begins, devoted to the occult and the pseudo-sciences. Flaubert, attached to reason and logic, had no time for the paranormal; but topics like 'magnetism' and hypnosis, by raising the central question of the relations between matter and spirit, rational and irrational interpretations of man and the world, offered a neat transition to philosophy and religion. Flaubert perpetrated here some of his most blatantly grotesque jokes, such as the anticlimactic outcome of the attempt to summon demons, when mysterious noises turn out to emanate from the terrified housekeeper. Yet he also, disconcertingly, gives Bouvard a gift for hypnotism, and successes with the medical exploitation of 'magnetic fields'. Coming back, with philosophy proper, into the ambit of their creator, the two clowns no longer merely read and do, they also think and feel. A dialogue between the materialist (Bouvard) and the spiritualist ends in a draw; a reading of extracts from Spinoza (one of Flaubert's favourite thinkers) has them all but lose their grip on reality.

Turning to less abstruse sources, they resume their duel, sure-footedly skipping from Locke to Descartes and from the origins of ideas to the faculties of the soul. They meet contradiction and absurdity as usual, but their questions now concern the human condition, so a new seriousness and tension are present. Their arguments with the *curé* and other local personalities have a sharper edge, as both are drawn to philosophical nihilism, denying free will, morality, providence, principles. The villagers, wounded also by 'their evident superiority', invent calumnies about them:

> Then a pitiable faculty developed in their mind: that of seeing stupidity and tolerating it no longer. Insignificant things made them sad: newspaper advertisements, the silhouette of a bourgeois, a stupid reflexion overheard by chance. (. . .) They no longer went out, admitted no-one. (VIII)

Their gloom and inactivity are more complete than after the *coup d'état*: which perhaps establishes the relative superiority of philosophy over politics in Flaubert's own hierarchy of values. Stumbling on the rotting corpse of a dog, they consider death as the final proof of the absurdity of life. In a passage of genuine sombre lyricism they decide to commit suicide and coolly choose their method. When the day comes, Flaubert insists on the physiological and even petty circumstantial factors triggering the act itself: not so much a devaluation of existential choice as a true novelist's insistence on the complexity of man, and a demonstration of the impossibility of separating spirit from matter. Impossible also, for Flaubert to imagine life without chance: a chance reminds the pair that they have forgotten to make a will, another reminds them that it is Christmas and draws them, out of curiosity, to the church, where the special atmosphere of the festival and the patent conviction of the large congregation suggest that religion may offer a positive and satisfying explanation of life.

For his old bachelors as for his spinster Félicité, Flaubert the novelist is willing to suspend if not his disbelief at least his derision; but not his perception of contradiction and intellectual dishonesty. Hence in search of balm for their disappointed spirits, the couple find the Old Testament far less congenial than the Gospels. Temperamental differences, as usual, affect their responses. Bouvard at first drags his feet, while Pécuchet is soon absorbed in extreme asceticism, eventually drawing his friend after him. Their rising involvement in religion is finally brought down only by the failure of truly mystical experiences to manifest themselves. In Pécuchet's case there is also a need for assurance to be accompanied by knowledge, and he gradually begins to see biblical and doctrinal incoherences and the circular arguments used by the parish priest to fudge them over. Once more the modestly-endowed character becomes an authorial mouthpiece as the shadow of Saint Antoine falls over the text:

> Pécuchet became a student of myth (. . .)
> He compared the Virgin to Isis, the eucharist to the Persian Homa, Bacchus to Moses, Noah's Ark to Xisuthros' boat: these similarities for him demonstrated that all religions were the same. (IX)

But Flaubert drew back from giving Pécuchet a superior intellectual status. Though he plunged him next into the study of martyrdom (shades of *Trois Contes*!) he set the discussion with the priest in the absurd context of a downpour which not only forces the adversaries to share the same umbrella but also ironically inflicts a mild torture on them! Finally Pécuchet drifts away from Catholicism, partly because he cannot reconcile faith and reason and partly because he cannot stomach the conservative, politicised religion of the local aristocracy. Yet when the two bachelors observe the Félicité-like devotions of their half-witted servant Marcel, it is Pécuchet who defends him:

> What does the belief matter? The important thing is to believe. (IX)

A series of neatly interwoven episodes leads from religion to education. A second narrative cycle seems to be beginning as the learners teach. The unfinished Chapter X has four functions. Educational theories are tried out; there is a miniature recapitulation of the whole novel in the range of subjects the pair tackle; some new fields of knowledge – such as music and botany – are added, while digressions bring in urbanism and the legal system, with hints that the pair have evolved into Socialism; finally the underlying message is that whatever the system adopted or the skills of the teachers, education succeeds only if the pupils are by nature teachable. Given the constant pessimistic twist of Flaubert's psychological determinism, it is not surprising that Victor and Victorine, children of a criminal and a fecklessly amoral peasant woman, effortlessly 'conquer' all attempts to cultivate them. Furthermore, the two teachers, despite frequent earlier glimmerings of superiority and acquired understanding, seem to be no more practically competent nor intellectually secure than in Chapter II: Pécuchet's enthusiastic efforts to teach music are incoherent and unreasonably demanding. Gothot-Mersch rightly points out that, having learned nothing, they cannot teach.[35] The plans show that the pair would next try to teach the adults, an even more absurd enterprise in Flaubert's eyes. A minor riot was to have resulted, followed by a philosophical dialogue in which Bouvard's scientific and technical optimism would have been opposed by Pécuchet's pessimistic vision of the future.

The plans for Chapter XI explain and describe the return to copying. Feeling that everything has gone to pieces in their hands, the heroes abandon practical action and active study for mere reproduction of other people's words. 'Let us work without reasoning', says Candide's pragmatic friend Martin. Flaubert's echo is partial, distorted to fit his own verbal concept of 'work'. Voltaire's protagonists literally cultivate their garden, and, he adds, 'The small piece of land gave a large yield'. Critics have noted that since Bouvard and Pécuchet now copy together, at a special double desk, they have at least conquered the solitude which characterised their earlier working lives: unlike, one might add, the hermit of Croisset. But this mechanical process marks a new beginning. They pick up contradictions and absurdities in their reading, and group their extracts under specific headings to bring these out, just as Flaubert had done in the novel proper. In a third stage of awareness they compile the celebrated *Dictionary of Received Ideas*, a guide to all the appropriate things the 'bourgeois' should think or say. Having collected material since 1850, Flaubert had amassed nearly a thousand entries. These are not quotations, but definitions of key words, summaries of key ideas and instructions on how to use them, on how much, or rather how little, the bourgeois needs to know. They suppose a higher level of sophistication on the part of Bouvard and Pécuchet than the copying stages.

Eventually, though, as so often already, the sheer complexity and heterogeneity of material was to defy their ordering process and they were to go back yet again to automatic copying. As if this were not enough cycles within cycles, in Chapter XII they find a letter in which the local doctor offers the Prefect of the Department his considered diagnosis of his strange neighbours: 'mad but harmless'.

Of the letter, Flaubert noted:

> Summarising all their actions and thoughts it must be, for the reader, a criticism of the novel. (Folio edition, p. 443)

After a discussion, the pair copy the letter. In so doing, of course, they may be argued to be reducing the 'criticism' to the same dubious status as the other texts they copy; and Flaubert's plan was to overwhelm the reader by reproducing the others, too, as a massive anthology of daft quotations for all occasions, at the end of the book. But perhaps the real importance of the letter, for a novelist who had so often used shifting point of view as a means of undermining the reader's confidence in his grasp of the 'certitudes' of a text, lay in the sudden re-interpretation of the conduct of the two 'seekers-after-truth'.[36] His other novels all end with a simpler version of the same device: Charles Bovary's 'It's the fault of fatality'; the Carthaginian praise of Salammbô for bringing down Mâtho; Frédéric and Deslauriers recalling 'the best thing that ever happened' to them. As in many modern novels, from Proust onwards, the reader is invited to go back to the beginning, to re-read the text, in which he will not only be able to test the new hypothesis but also have the opportunity of finding other perspectives.

Unfortunately, the letter itself was never written. Flaubert's tantalising note, like the whole plan for the conclusion, as well as the 'anti-novelistic' aspects of the completed text, hint at his inventive modernity.[37] *Mise en abyme* (the miniature reproduction of a work within the work itself), self-reflexivity, the self-critical text, circular or spiral forms, the use of explicit quotation and 'intertextuality', the deliberate undermining of the distinction between fact and fiction, the accumulation of unresolved 'loose ends' in the fiction itself, all these features flourish in the modern experimental novel. But the note also reminds the reader of what, in the completed text, Flaubert had sacrificed to make room for his 'philosophical tale', his assault on nineteenth-century knowledge and its practitioners. He has, compared to his earlier fiction, curtailed his exploration of the inner life and of interpersonal and social relations. The psychological interest of the protagonists is intermittent, and that of the secondary characters extremely sketchy. Inner monologue, free indirect speech, character analysis, the interplay of viewpoints and the subtle placing of the reader in an equivocally privileged position where he can at once feel with and observe the characters, are sacrificed to the document, the summary or the comic effect, the semi-erudite argument or the facile deflating juxtaposition. The sacrifice does not always seem justified.

Many of Flaubert's targets are 'soft' – mediocre vulgarisers or outdated 'authorities' – while major writers or thinkers are 'picked off' by a careful choice which isolates weakness or apparent absurdities from the whole body of an argument. Flaubert's own voracious reading had made him an intellectual 'jack of all trades', but he had no specialised training. Master only of writing itself, he could in other fields apply only basic logic and commonsense as critical tools. Developments in many of the domains he so dismissively treated a century ago have suggested that these tools are not up to the task of demolition to which they were put. If his characters can make nothing of elementary atomic theory, how would they – or he – cope with anti-matter? Furthermore, while the protagonists' naïvety is a powerful critical weapon, their lack of patience, their hasty dilettantism, often blunt its effect, leaving the reader unsure whether Flaubert himself had actually decided on the role his protagonists should be playing *vis à vis* the theme of knowledge.

Even with the benefits of scholarship then, the 'message' of this extended philosophical tale remains uncertain. To the modern reader it is as if Flaubert's Enlightenment model was not after all the limpidity of Voltaire but the clouded, deliberately-turbulent waters of Diderot, who, like Flaubert, preferred paradoxes to conclusions, open ended dialogue to synthesis, and who also practised a kind of deliberately puzzling 'anti-novel'.[38] Though Flaubert's characters – and their printed sources, often reproduced as passages of quasi-quotation in the present tense – are left to condemn themselves in their own words, there are even fewer signs than usual of the author's standpoint as expressed through the narratorial voice. A leading Flaubert scholar, while fairly sure that his target is 'the ridiculous pretention of those who think they know', is inclined to extend this category to the whole of nineteenth-century science; and indeed she quotes a manuscript note in which Flaubert expressed his intention of proving to his heroes 'that it is impossible to know the Truth'.[39] A recent critic observes that the novel 'not only resists all reader-effort to recuperate meaning, it foregrounds that resistance and makes it its very subject'.[40]

But just how negative is the novel? Quotations from Flaubert's own works were to figure in the reproduced dossier of copy, alongside other writers he admired.[41] But it is difficult to believe that even in the most depressed moments of his final years he can have felt that this inclusion disqualified the whole body of his writings from the serious attention of the intelligent reader. Perhaps his final lesson was one not of nihilism but of humility. Humility and obstinacy. His characters' refusal to give in, their remarkable resilience, are surely as striking as their thirty failures, and faithfully echo, in the comic mode as usual, a central feature of their creator. For throughout the period of composition of this novel, seen by many recent critics as the book to end all books, Flaubert was not preparing a smug retirement from a profession he had rendered redundant. On the contrary he was collecting ideas for his next novel, and the one after that. In 1853 he had written that 'ink is my natural element' (Plé. II, 395), and to the end he never renounced what was to him not only a personal necessity, like the air he breathed, but a service to others.

9
The Critical Heritage

A great writer satisfies more than one demand, replies to more
than one doubt, nourishes a variety of appetites. (Gide)

Interpretation and criticism of Flaubert over 130 years have shown
the richness of his work by the variety of appetites, doubts and
demands they have satisfied. They have also often illustrated the
weaknesses which he himself castigated in the criticism, thought
and use of language of his own day.

From the start there was diversity, even contradiction, partly
nourished by Flaubert's own strategies, especially the revolutionary
principle of 'impassibility', and by his implicit theory of the active,
participatory reader. The vast majority of his earliest reviewers and
critics had neither the skill nor the time to read his works as closely
as he required. They dismissed them as boring, immoral, artless (!),
banal in subject-matter and devoid of all feeling and of all literary
skills except that of obstinate description.

Creative writers were from the start more perceptive, though, like
Baudelaire in 1857, always inclined to highlight those features which
fitted their own vision or aesthetic principles. Thus Zola, the first of
many to see Flaubert as a precursor, a 'modern', projected an image
of him as the father of the documentary and scientific novel, praising
the ordinariness of his plots and his modern-day protagonists, and
the painstaking reconstitutions involved in his historical works.
Absorbed in a utilitarian view of literature, Zola neglected both
Flaubert's craftsmanship and his obsession with Art and aesthetic
values.[42] Flaubert's only disciple, Maupassant, was almost alone in
seeking to balance the question of his 'realism' against his concept
of the novel as work of art, his pursuit of beauty and perfection and
his acute sense that writing was a craft, a skill in the careful handling
of words. Maupassant fought against the view that a Flaubert text

was just a piling up of 'facts' and observations, and made the first revelations about his elaborate working methods. He also insisted on Flaubert's Romantic temperament and tastes, revealing that the master of sober modern realism felt more at home in the literature of excess, and reminding his readers that Flaubert was also the author of *La Tentation de Saint Antoine*.[43] The very early publication of selections from Flaubert's correspondence (1884-93) helped to highlight the complexities evoked by Maupassant, illustrating the diverse and contradictory nature of his personality and ideas. The indiscretions of his friend du Camp, who revealed that he had for years suffered from fits, not only opened up a rich subject to biographical controversy, it also suggested an artistic temperament at once less controlled and controllable than Maupassant's picture, an idea which would be taken up later by Freudians and others.

The first published letters shed particular light on the strength of Flaubert's feelings, studiously concealed in his fiction, and especially on his revulsion from the ugliness and stupidity he found everywhere in the modern world. Thus by 1893 Henry James[44] had pinned down a key paradox:

> Impersonal as he wished his work to be, it was his strange fortune to be the most expansive, the most vociferous, the most spontaneous of men.

It was also James who coined the expression 'the novelist's novelist' in appreciation of the high level of conscious artistry Flaubert had brought to a literary genre hitherto marked primarily by amateurism or haste. But it was also James who first expressed some of the major reservations about Flaubert's achievement which have continued to carry weight. He wrote of 'a tenacity in the void of a life laid down for grammar'; regretted that Flaubert's abhorrence of the bourgeois seemed to fill his horizon and prevent him from writing about anything else; and above all condemned Flaubert's choice, for the central point of view in his novels, of 'such limited reflectors and registers of the world' as Emma or Frédéric. These reservations were to surface mainly in Anglo-Saxon criticism, in the work of Lubbock or Turnell, for example, who dismiss the psychological value of the novels or consider Flaubert's vision a regrettable survival of facile adolescent pessimism.[45]

Turnell and others have also more or less explicitly regretted the absence of a firm moral standpoint, forgetting that all the great French *moralistes* have tended to be de-moralisers, portraying the realities of human nature to explode the simplifications or hypocrisies of dominant moral codes of behaviour, which they will at most propose replacing with a pragmatic *modus vivendi*.

French commentators, for their part, have long taken seriously Flaubert's psychological insights. By 1892 Jules de Gaultier[46] had built up an elaborate theory of mental processes and attitudes to the world which he called *bovarysme*: the capacity given to man to conceive himself as other than he really is. The very word *bovarysme* is symptomatic of an important feature of Flaubert studies, the narrowing of focus onto a single work which even today attracts the bulk of critical attention. Despite Maupassant, the works which did not fit 'realist' modes of fiction, psychological or social, were neglected for long periods, and even *L'Education Sentimentale* and *Bouvard et Pécuchet* embarrassed many unconditional admirers of Flaubert's first published novel.

It seemed difficult to fit Flaubert's career into the favoured pattern of a stately progress to maturity of thought and perfection of form. In the 1920s, Thibaudet tried to apply Bergson's influential theory of the flux of consciousness to Flaubert's career, seeing in it an alternation of the products of distinct impulses, which gave both works of 'ironic observation' and works of 'decorative imagination'.[47] Thibaudet also inaugurated the close study of Flaubert's style, after a trenchant article from Marcel Proust[48] had drawn his attention to some of the subtleties of Flaubert's use of the basic parts of speech, especially the tenses of the verb. Thibaudet pioneered the combination of a close reading of Flaubert's correspondence with detailed analysis of his works, showing for example the strengths and weaknesses resulting from the novelist's phobia about the accumulation of relative pronouns.

Many later stylistic studies of Flaubert have built on Thibaudet's insights, supplemented in the case of his imagery (neglected or undervalued by Proust and Thibaudet) by the monumental study undertaken by Demorest.[49]

Scholarly work was also being published on the details of Flaubert's life and character, notably by Descharmes and Dumesnil. The juvenilia had appeared at last almost in full (1910) as had the travel notes (1910, 1927); and from 1934 manuscripts of the major works entered public archives, making possible the study of their genesis. Though as yet only that of *Madame Bovary* has been the subject of a book,[50] theses, monographs and modern annotated editions have all explored the dossiers, plans and manuscript drafts. The aim is partly to establish the processes of composition, sources of inspiration, and so on, and partly to shed light on the structure and meaning of the completed works. In some cases this scholarship has been instrumental in completely re-situating a text, perhaps most obviously with *La Tentation de Saint Antoine*, considered an outpouring of Flaubert's suspect imagination until research showed even his wildest or most grotesque passages to be rooted in impeccable scholarly sources. More recently scholars have used the sources of *Salammbô* to question the author's claim to documentary precision and affirm that his careful selections and re-working of material owes more to his artistic vision, and perhaps his psyche, than to the principles of historiography.[51]

Flaubert's claims to the status of historian – of the past or of his own time – have naturally caught the interest of Marxist critics, who judge imaginative literature largely in terms of its value as history. Lukács in his influential study *The Historical Novel* (1947) was typical of the early dogmatic approach. He considered that after the defeat of the 1848 Revolution, France's bourgeois writers had turned away from the valuable 'critical realism' which had characterised Balzac's perception of the contradictions of early nineteenth-century capitalism, and had wasted their time in the study of the subjectivity of the exceptional individual. As he rightly observed, Flaubert's hatred of the bourgeois, being accompanied by contempt for the common people, had no roots in the 'great popular democratic traditions', and thus had no constructive value.

Indeed many of Flaubert's principles make him a difficult subject for a Marxist approach: his refusal to synthesise, to offer a coherent picture, his scepticism and pessimism about man and society, his distrust of ideologies, and above all his cyclic view of history, as reflected in the macrocosm of *La Tentation*, at the national level in *Salammbô* or in the microcosm of the lives of his nineteenth-century 'heroes'. Post-war Marxists have nonetheless been more ready to evaluate positively a writer who does so fully represent a key moment of contradiction and complexity in bourgeois thought: that dialectical overreaction to the defeat of the Republican hopes of the 1840s which plunged the artist into aestheticism and his major characters into hopeless despair.[52]

The inevitable complement of Marx, in twentieth-century images of Man, has been Freud, explorer of the structures not of society but of the psyche. Flaubert's notoriously quirky character and lifestyle and his complex-ridden protagonists could not fail to attract psychoanalysis. Despite the protests of conventional biographers, who feel obliged to seek directly 'readable' evidence before making claims about their subjects' formative years, psychoanalytical commentators have detected in Flaubert a variety of syndromes, from the Oedipus complex to the frustration of the infant rejected by its mother.

The works have generally been used to probe Flaubert's own unconscious, though a recent *Psychoanalytical Reading* of *Madame Bovary*[53] traces the importance of the primal scene – in this case deprivation of maternal love – through the life of the protagonist. Because the Freudian analysis is based both on the deviations that the conscious mind imposes on unconscious impulses, and on the moments when the unconscious breaks through, the lack of hard evidence about the infancy of Flaubert or Emma poses no problem. Freud's idea that therapy is a 'talking-out' of repressions via the unconscious ambiguities of language used by the older patient provides a model for the critic's method as, armed with the master's guide to symbolic meanings, he tracks his way through Flaubert's texts, which are conveniently at once highly-wrought and enigmatic.

In both Freudian and Marxist approaches, the imposition of a neat, closed system of references on a notably open and polyvalent text may irritate the uncommitted reader, aware of how much else is being swept aside or overlooked. One solution much favoured by French critics has been precisely to combine the Freudian with the Marxist models, and even add something home-grown such as existentialism or phenomenology. Sartre's voluminous but unfinished study[54] does this, exploring simultaneously Flaubert's relations with his family, his class and his times: in one purple passage Gustave is made to see the victorious Bismarck of 1870 as a double of his own feared and hated father, or to be more precise the father-type of Sartre's chosen Freudian model.

Whatever one makes of the neat, and yet apparently infinitely variable pattern-building of these approaches, their value has been twofold: to bring back into serious consideration long-neglected works such as the juvenilia, *La Tentation* or *Salammbô*, and to reassert

Flaubert's importance as an explorer of human nature and the individual in society. The latter has proved a particularly valuable counterweight to the extreme implications of another modern school of criticism.

Structuralism started from two postulates of the linguist Saussure (1857–1913): that there is only a conventional link between the word and the thing, and that a language is a coherent and autonomous system of signs. It developed the view that all meaning consists of closed systems, independent of the material world, our perception of which is ultimately controlled by language itself. A work of literature, because it does not refer directly to real people and events, is a particularly valuable phenomenon for structuralists. It is indeed a paradigm of the autonomy of the system, further remarkable by its measure of self-awareness as a system, since it is always a more or less carefully elaborated construct. The role of the critic is to establish the key features or structures. There is much in this approach, which starts with the text itself, that echoes Flaubert's own ideal of criticism.

In an important letter of 1869 he attacked the extraneous criteria applied by Classicism (rhetorical rules) or Romanticism (biography or history), calling for an 'inscient poetics', focused on 'the work itself', a study of 'its composition, its style' (VI, 8). However, structuralism in its purest form tended to throw out two of Flaubert's central principles: 'representation', and what he called in the same letter 'the point of view of the author'. It tended to claim that the main, perhaps even the only, theme of literature should be the particular qualities of language itself and especially the deconstruction of the illusory 'realisms' which are the result of man's failure to grasp that his language constructs, and does not neutrally reflect, the world around him. While acutely aware that certain languages – what he called *idées reçues* – did exactly this, Flaubert remained convinced that the writer's language could and should be different. On the other hand, the structuralists' reasoned abolition of the traditional separation of form from content is very much in line with Flaubert's own definition of style, quoted in Chapter 3.

Structuralists have not had the monopoly of close textual analysis of Flaubert since the war. Another of the themes of Flaubert's own reflexions on language has been taken up by several generations of critics: the idea that prose should aspire to qualities analogous to those possessed by poetry. His novels and stories are now often read as poems, the quest for patterns of theme, imagery or symbol being preferred to the traditional analysis of the development of the story or the interaction of the characters. Though homing in on 'structures', Poulet, Richard or Brombert are far from seeking to abolish the author; indeed their main purpose is to establish links between his perception of the self and the world and the precise configuration of his writing. Poulet starts from a minute exploration of a short text which seems to contain a fundamental insight; further examples are sought in other passages, in the pattern of a novel, across the works as a whole; and supporting evidence is invoked from the correspondence. Flaubert *and* all his major characters are thus shown, through the obsessive return of the images of circles, to be haunted by the reality of constriction while longing to participate in a movement of expansion. As a consequence of his insight into the true nature of human consciousness, argues Poulet, Flaubert is obliged to dissolve away the traditional linearity and continuity of narrative fiction.[55]

Rousset, meanwhile, focusses on one of Flaubert's major techniques, the way he modulates the narrative viewpoint, literally leading the reader's eye from one viewing character to another and into their respective consciousnesses, rarely interposing his (or the narrator's) own. 'Inner vision' and 'immobility', Flaubert's central themes for Rousset, are seen once again as incompatible with the novel proper.[56]

These and other new versions of Zola's old idea that Flaubert was the first of the moderns because he abandoned certain established features of the genre have broadly coincided with the rise of the French 'new novel'. A number of experimental writers consciously set out during the 1950s to undermine such traditional features as plot, the coherent character, social significance and the distinction between form and content. Furthermore, in seeming to replace these features by massive blocks of obstinate description, by attempts to communicate the nuances of an elusive and amorphous consciousness, or by complex and often obscure variations of narrative voice and point of view; in stressing the importance of the subjective perception of time or space and the role of memory; in building elaborate verbal patterns of theme or image; above all, perhaps, in making extraordinary new demands on the patience and perspicacity of their readers, novels by Robbe-Grillet or Sarraute, Butor or Simon recalled the works of Flaubert, not infrequently acknowledged as a 'precursor'. Some critics of the period reexamined his works in this context. Thus Bollème[57] saw Flaubert as striving at once to assert the autonomy of inanimate things and the way the consciousness perceives them and gives them meaning in relation to its own desires or memories. These emotionally-charged descriptions became the core of the work, functioning as a new way of involving the reader to replace the old attractions of conventional narrative such as 'what happens next'.

Gérard Genette[58] broadly agreed that the importance of Flaubert lay in certain privileged moments of contemplation evoked by purely descriptive passages. However, in the face of the evidence of the texts themselves, which do after all tell a story, and of the drafts, correspondences and innumerable other documents which trace Flaubert's abiding concern with this and the other 'traditional' features of the genre, he was more circumspect than Bollème, concluding ambiguously that:

> Flaubert never stopped writing novels, while refusing the demands of discourse proper to the novel,

It is this paradox which exercises the ingenuity – and challenges the intellectual honesty – of modern critical approaches to Flaubert. Not every recent commentator has been willing to write that 'Flaubert's art is continually one of compromise', as does Sherrington,[59] when his detailed study of modern techniques of point of view reveal the continuing, if discreet, presence of an old-fashioned narrator's voice in passages of psychological analysis, generalisation or personal intervention. The simple fact remains that however intuitively prescient about the psyche or the nature of language, however much a precursor of the 'new novel', Flaubert wrote his fiction between 1850 and 1880 and belongs *also* to the nineteenth-century tradition. It has become fashionable to present Flaubert's relation to it as merely an artful and knowing 'deconstruction' of its codes and conventions, especially through parody; but this is at once an overreaction to earlier neglect of traditional features, and a simplification. Flaubert does like to mock his contemporaries; but he also at times writes like them because he wants to do essentially the same kinds of things as them: to illustrate a 'point of view' on the human condition by telling a story. It is indeed the survival of this traditional element which allows Flaubert to appeal at once to the general reader of fiction and to the practitioner and the critic of its most modern, and often most arcane and hermetic, developments, who may at times seem to be writing only for each other.

*

Recent work on Flaubert has been marked not only by extraordinary variety but also by a sometimes bewildering eclecticism. For example, it is not surprising that the structuralist obsession with language should cross-fertilise with recent developments in the 'new novel' to awaken an interest in word play in Flaubert, as manifest in his choice of proper names or the patterning of certain sound-clusters. It is rather more surprising to find such considerations in a wide-ranging exercise in comparative literature exploring the novel form's use of adultery to launch an attack on social and moral values.[60] Other critics have tired of circular arguments about language and resurrected referentiality, for example by considering anew *Flaubert's Characters*[61] or by making his lifelong interest in myth and religion the focus of a study which proposes that even his realistic, apparently secular, novels be read as thinly-disguised restatements of that interest.[62] Freudian approaches have been rejuvenated by strong doses of his linguistically-biased French successor and adapter, Jacques Lacan,[63] while Marxist or other socio-historical readings now show strong feminist overtones.[64]

Scholarship, meanwhile, has not yet digested the mountains of manuscripts – some relating to *L'Education Sentimentale* surfaced only in 1975. The trend now is to fuller variant editions and even 'diplomatic' transcriptions: a single chapter of *Madame Bovary* occupies, with its explanatory commentary, two volumes![65] Even without the 'benefits' offered by this record of every change of mind, purple passages like this one (the *comices agricoles*) and puzzle-pages like the first-person opening to the same novel or the final paragraphs of *L'Education Sentimentale* continue to generate both intelligent and thought-provoking, but still not exhaustive, *explications* and wild and carelessly-documented theories. At least, serious doubters of the school of Henry James seem to have been drowned in the chorus of admiration, as even 'a life laid down for grammar' now constitutes, for many critics, the highest possible praise.

Since Flaubert both saw himself as a divided and contradictory personality and wrote in a way deliberately intended to challenge and puzzle, it is no doubt highly appropriate that the critical approaches brought to bear on his works should continue to diversify. But as Flaubert was a careful, conscientious and comprehensive craftsman, it is also appropriate that critical reading of the texts be marked by the same characteristics. As Flaubert hated the cliché and exploded the hollowness of the jargon of his own time, it is regrettable that many contemporary critics allow the sound of their own jargon to drown the creator's unique voice. In his own last works, Flaubert found a way of tempering pride and persistence with modesty and even humility, a lesson that not all his critics have taken to heart.

Notes

1. The two-volume *Oeuvres Complètes* (Paris: Seuil, l'Intégrale, 1964) reproduces most of these, including thirty-one literary titles and three travel-works written before 1850. For a detailed study of the pre-1845 texts, see J. Bruneau, *Les Débuts littéraires de Gustave Flaubert* (Paris: Armand Colin, 1962).

2. Bruneau, *op. cit.* p. 187.

3. Flaubert, *Souvenirs, Notes et Pensées Intimes* (Paris: Buchet-Chastel, 1965), p. 110.

4. Bruneau, *op. cit.* p. 285.

5. Flaubert, *op. cit.* pp. 109–11.

6. *Ibid*, p. 109.

7. See Ch. 3.

8. The pair wrote alternate chapters of *Par les Champs et Par les Grèves*. Flaubert's chapters were first published in 1886 and appear in *Oeuvres Complètes* (Paris: Seuil, l'Intégrale, 1964) II, pp. 472–549.

9. See the studies by J. Seznec: *Les Sources de l'Episode des Dieux dans 'La Tentation de Saint Antoine'* (Paris: Vrin, 1940) and *Nouvelles études sur 'La Tentation de Saint Antoine'* (London: Warburg Institute, 1949).

10. T. Unwin, 'Flaubert's first *Tentation de Saint-Antoine*', *Essays in French Literature*, XVI, Nov. 1979, p. 18.

11. For a detailed psychoanalytical study, see J. Bem, *Désir et Savoir dans l'oeuvre de Flaubert. Etude de 'La Tentation de Saint Antoine'* (Neuchâtel: A la Baconnière, 1979).

12. The *Préface* to Bouilhet's *Dernières Chansons* is reprinted in *Oeuvres Complètes* (Paris: Seuil, l'Intégrale, 1964) II, pp. 759–64.

13. A. Fairlie, *Flaubert: Madame Bovary* (London: Edward Arnold, 1962), p. 12.

14. Baudelaire's review can be read in *L'Art Romantique* (Paris: Garnier-Flammarion, 1968), pp. 219–228.

15. M. Tillett, *On reading Flaubert* (London: Oxford University Press, 1961), pp. 15–16.

16. James' essays of 1893 and 1902 are reprinted in *Selected Literary Criticism* (ed. M. Shapira. Harmondsworth: Penguin, 1963). Lawrence's strictures can be found in *Phoenix* (London: Heinemann, 1961), p. 226.

17. Baudelaire, *art.cit.*, p. 227.

18. L. Bersani, 'The Narrator and the bourgeois community in *Madame*

Bovary', *French Review*, May 1959, pp. 527–33. Considerably developed by A. Raitt, 'Nous étions à l'étude' in *Flaubert 2. Mythes et Religions, La Revue des Lettres Modernes*, 1986, pp. 161–192.

19. D. A. Williams, 'Generalizations in *Madame Bovary'*, *Neophilologus*, Oct.1978, pp. 492–503.

20. See R. Pascal, *The Dual Voice* (Manchester University Press, 1977) for a study of this technique, and an extensive bibliography.

21. For example, V. Brombert, 'An epic of immobility' *Hudson Review*, spring 1966, pp. 24–43.

22. For example, J. Bem, 'Modernité de *Salammbô'*, *Littérature*, Dec.1980, pp. 18–31.

23. N. Schor, *Breaking the chain: women, theory and French realist fiction* (New York: Columbia University Press, 1985), Ch. 6.

24. See the new Classiques Garnier edition of the novel (ed. P. Wetherill) and the same editor's companion volume, called *L'Education Sentimentale. Images et Documents* (Paris: Garnier, 1985).

25. R. J. Sherrington in *Three Novels by Flaubert. A study of techniques* (Oxford: Clarendon Press, 1970), Ch. V, argues that Frédéric's passion is a figment of his imagination.

26. Flaubert based this triangular relationship on his own with Maurice and Elisa Schlesinger.

27. Many critics have contrasted the role of chance here to the strong sense of determinism, even fatality, given by the structure of *Madame Bovary*.

28. See Sherrington. *op. cit.*

29. The historical perspective is examined by several contributors to the collective volume *Histoire et Langage dans 'L'Education Sentimentale'* (Paris: S.E.D.E.S., 1981) and to the special number of *Europe* devoted to the novel (Sept.–Nov. 1969).

30. For example, M. G. Tillett, 'An approach to *Hérodias'*, *French Studies*, Jan. 1967, pp. 24–31.

31. For example, M. Sachs, 'Flaubert's *Trois Contes*. The reconquest of Art' and W. Jane Bancroft, 'Flaubert's *Légende de Saint Julien l'Hospitalier:* the duality of the artist-saint', in *Esprit Créateur*, spring 1970, pp. 62–74, 75-84.

32. Introduction to Harrap edition. p. 59.

33. F. J. Shepler, in 'La mort et la rédemption dans *Trois Contes* de Flaubert', *Neophilologus*, Oct. 1972, pp. 407–16, concludes that *Un coeur simple* records the loss of the powerful God of the other stories. P. Nykrog, in 'Les *Trois Contes* dans la structure thématique chez Flaubert', *Romantisme*, No.6 (1973), pp. 55–66, concludes that the three stories together seem to indicate signs of hope linked to a non-dogmatic Christianity.

34. Principally in editions of the novel by A. Cento (Paris: Nizet, 1964) and of the *Dictionnaire des Idées Reçues* by L. Caminiti (Paris: Nizet, 1966). The Folio edition contains the *Dictionnaire*, some plans and extracts from the quotations can be found in *Le second volume de Bouvard et Pécuchet*, ed. G. Bollème (Paris: Denoël, 1966), and a detailed transcription in a book of the same title, ed. A. Cento and L. Caminiti-Pennarola (Naples, 1981).

35. Introduction to Folio edition, p. 24.

36. He wrote in 1880: 'There is no Truth! There are only ways of

seeing. Is a photograph true to life?' (VIII, 370). And to Maupassant in 1878: 'Nothing is true but connections (*les rapports*), that is, the way we perceive objects'. (VIII, 135).

37. Flaubert himself wrote that 'Those who read a book to find out whether the baroness will marry the viscount are going to be fooled'. (VIII, 336).

38. To judge by the correspondence, Flaubert himself had little knowledge of Diderot's writings, whose rediscovery is largely a twentieth-century phenomenon.

39. Introduction to Folio edition, pp. 20–22.

40. S. Haig, *Flaubert and the gift of speech* (Cambridge University Press, 1984), p. 166.

41. Introduction to Folio edition, p. 42.

42. Zola's various articles are collected in *Oeuvres Complètes* X–XII (Paris: Cercle du Livre Précieux, 1968–9).

43. Maupassant's articles are collected in *Chroniques* I–III (Paris: 10–18, 1980).

44. See above, no.16.

45. P. Lubbock, *The Craft of Fiction* (London: Cape, 1921), M. Turnell, *The Novel in France* (London: Hamish Hamilton, 1950).

46. Notably in his philosophical essay *Le Bovarysme* (Paris: Le Cerf, 1892).

47. Thibaudet's study, *Gustave Flaubert*, first published in 1922, revised in 1935, is still in print (Paris: Gallimard).

48. First published in 1920. See M. Proust, *Contre Sainte-Beuve* (Paris: Pléiade, 1971), pp. 586–600.

49. D. L. Demorest, *L'Expression figurée et symbolique dans l'oeuvre de Gustave Flaubert* (Paris: les Presses Modernes, 1931).

50. C. Gothot-Mersch, *La Genèse de Madame Bovary* (Paris: Corti, 1966). A transcription of the draft manuscripts, made by G. Leleu, appeared as early as 1936.

51. Notably in a thesis (Toronto, 1974) and several articles by I. R. Strong. In a letter to an expert, Flaubert admitted, 'Besides, I can't any longer distinguish in my book the conjectures from the authentic sources'. (Sup. I, 307).

52. See, for example, E. Fischer, *The Necessity of Art* (Harmondsworth; Pelican, 1963) pp. 76–7.

53. By Ion K. Collas (Geneva: Droz, 1985).

54. *L'Idiot de la Famille* I–III (Paris: Gallimard, 1971–2).

55. G. Poulet, *Les Métamorphoses du Cercle* (Paris: Plon, 1961) Ch. XIII.

56. J. Rousset, *Forme et Signification* (Paris: Corti, 1962) Ch. V. For a useful corrective to these 'smash and grab' approaches to the texts, compare L. Bopp, *Commentaire sur 'Madame Bovary'* (Neuchâtel: A la Baconnière, 1951), a page by page analysis.

57. G. Bollème, *La Leçon de Flaubert* (Paris: Julliard, 1964).

58. G. Genette, *Figures I* (Paris: Seuil, 1966) pp. 223–43.

59. R. J. Sherrington, *Three Novels by Flaubert. A study of techniques* (Oxford: Clarendon Press, 1970).

60. T. Tanner, *Adultery in the Novel: Contract and Transgression* (Baltimore, London: John Hopkins University Press, 1979).

Gustave Flaubert

61. By D. Knight (Cambridge University Press, 1985).

62. M. Lowe, *Towards the real Flaubert* (Oxford: Clarendon Press, 1984).

63. See, for example, M. Robert, *En haine du roman. Etude sur Flaubert* (Paris: Balland, 1982).

64. L. Czyba, *Mythes et Idéologies de la Femme dans les romans de Flaubert* (Lyon: Presses Universitaires, 1983).

65. *Les Comices Agricoles*. Edited by J. Goldin (Geneva: Droz, 1984).

Select Bibliography

The most accessible edition of the full range of Flaubert's writings, correspondence apart, is the compact two-volume *Oeuvres Complètes* (Seuil, l'Intégrale, 1964). The sixteen volume *Oeuvres Complètes* edited by M. Bardèche (1971-6) includes the correspondence and reproduces some manuscript material. Cheap editions of the major works are available from Folio, Garnier-Flammarion and Livre de Poche. The Folio versions of *Salammbô* (ed. P. Moreau, 1970), *La Tentation de Saint Antoine* and *Bouvard et Pécuchet* (ed. C. Gothot-Mersch, 1983 and 1979) have useful prefaces and notes. The new Garnier-Flammarion edition of the 1869 *Education Sentimentale* (ed. C. Gothot-Mersch, 1985) offers much help with its complexities and historical allusions. Harrap publish *Madame Bovary* with an English introduction (by M. Overstall, and C. Duckworth's invaluably-annotated edition of *Trois Contes*. Apart from the Conard and Pléiade editions mentioned in the *Note on References,* a selection of Flaubert's letters has been made by G. Bollème: *Préface à la vie d'écrivain* (1963).

Many of Flaubert's peculiar qualities as a writer seem to evaporate under the translator's pen. Accurate English translations of the mature works are available in Penguin Classics, while the 1845 *Sentimental Education* is published by the University of California Press. Francis Steegmuller has translated two intelligent selections from the Correspondence for Faber.

The bibliography on Flaubert, like a miniature model of the expanding universe, increases at the rate of 200 items per year. The following selection, confined to books and concentrating where possible on those in English, includes some standard biographical or critical studies together with works on individual texts and examples of recent critical approaches. Most of them contain extensive bibliographies.

Bart, Benjamin F., *Flaubert* (New York: Syracuse University Press, 1967).
Bem, Jeanne, *Désir et Savoir dans l'oeuvre de Flaubert. Etude de La Tentation de Saint Antoine* (Neuchâtel: A la Baconnière, 1979).
Brombert, Victor, *Flaubert* (Paris: Seuil, 1971).
Brombert, Victor, *The Novels of Flaubert* (Princeton: Princeton University Press, 1966).
Bruneau, Jean, *Les Débuts littéraires de Gustave Flaubert* (Paris: Armand Colin, 1962).

Carlut, Charles, *La Correspondance de Flaubert. Etude et Répertoire critique* (Paris: A. G. Nizet, 1968).

Cogny, Pierre, *'L'Education Sentimentale' de Flaubert* (Paris: Larousse, 1975).

Culler, Jonathan, *Flaubert. The Uses of Uncertainty* (London: Paul Elek, 1974).

Douchin, Jacques-Louis, *La Vie Erotique de Flaubert* (Paris: Carrère, 1984).

Fairlie, Alison, *Flaubert: Madame Bovary* (London: Edward Arnold, 1962).

Green, Anne, *Flaubert and the Historical Novel. 'Salammbô' reassessed* (Cambridge University Press, 1982).

Knight, Diana, *Flaubert's Characters* (Cambridge University Press, 1985).

Lowe, Margaret, *Towards the real Flaubert* (Oxford: Clarendon Press, 1984).

Nadeau, Maurice, *Gustave Flaubert, écrivain* (Paris: Les Lettres Nouvelles, 1969).

Robert, Marthe, *En haine du roman. Etude sur Flaubert* (Paris: Balland, 1982).

Sherrington, R. J., *Three Novels by Flaubert. A study of techniques* (Oxford: Clarendon Press, 1970).

Spica, Ingrid, *Le statut romanesque du 'Bouvard et Pécuchet' de Flaubert* (Manila: University of the Philippines, 1982).

Starkie, Enid, *Flaubert. The Making of the Master* (London: Weidenfeld and Nicolson, 1967).

Starkie, Enid, *Flaubert. The Master* (London: Weidenfeld and Nicolson, 1971).

Thibaudet, Albert, *Gustave Flaubert* (Paris: Gallimard, 1982).

Tillett, Margaret, *On reading Flaubert* (London: Oxford University Press, 1961).

Williams, D. A., *Psychological Determinism in 'Madame Bovary'* (University of Hull, 1973).

Williams, D. A., *The Hidden Life at its Source: a study of Flaubert's 'L'Education Sentimentale'*. (Hull University Press, 1987).

Index